TWENTIETH CENTURY
INTERPRETATIONS
OF
1984

TWENTIETH CENTURY
INTERPRETATIONS
OF
1984

A Collection of Critical Essays

Edited by
SAMUEL HYNES

Prentice-Hall, Inc. *Englewood Cliffs*, N. J.

A SPECTRUM BOOK

PRENTICE-HALL INTERNATIONAL, INC. (*London*)
PRENTICE-HALL OF AUSTRALIA, PTY. LTD. (*Sydney*)
PRENTICE-HALL OF CANADA, LTD. (*Toronto*)
PRENTICE-HALL OF INDIA PRIVATE LTD. (*New Delhi*)
PRENTICE-HALL OF JAPAN, INC. (*Tokyo*)

Contents

Herbert Read:
1984

Wyndham Lewis:
Climax and Change

A. L. Morton:
From *The English Utopia*

Chronology of Important Dates
Notes on the Editor and Contributors

TWENTIETH CENTURY
INTERPRETATIONS
OF
1984

Introduction

by Samuel Hynes

I

Some writers seem more important to us for what they have understood than for what they have achieved. In troubled times the man who can see a problem clearly, even if he cannot solve it, is valuable; and that was the kind of value that George Orwell had. He never wrote a book without flaws, and sometimes he wrote clumsily and badly, but he understood the problem of being human in the modern world and tried to express that understanding in his writing. One might put the problem, as Orwell saw it, in these terms: in this world, where social and political issues press in upon us with terrible urgency, how can a man live morally and responsibly and yet preserve a private self? For a serious artist like Orwell the problem has a particular form—how is art to play a significant role in our lives, and yet remain art? But he was also aware of its widest implications, the ways in which it affects us all; for what the question really asks is, how can the private life of the mind survive the pressures of the world outside? In that form, it is at the troubled center of contemporary life.

Orwell gave his own account of the problem in his essay "Why I Write":

> So long as I remain alive and well, I shall continue to feel strongly about prose style, to love the surface of the earth, and to take pleasure in solid objects and scraps of useless information. It is no use trying to suppress that side of myself. The job is to reconcile my ingrained likes and dislikes with the essentially public, non-individual activities that this age forces on all of us. It is not easy. It raises problems of construction and of language, and it raises in a new way the problem of truthfulness.[1]

To understand this passage properly, one must begin with "this age." Orwell's generation was the one born in the first decade of the twen-

---

[1] *The Collected Essays, Journalism and Letters of George Orwell*, ed. Sonia Orwell and Ian Angus (London: Martin Secker & Warburg Ltd., 1968), I, 6. Hereafter abbreviated *CEJL*. Further footnotes will be incorporated into the text. All quotations from Orwell's other books are from the first English editions.

tieth century. He and his contemporaries could just remember the Edwardian prewar world of security and peace. They were boys during the First World War, too young to fight in it, but old enough to know that their brothers and fathers were dying and to share in the postwar disillusionment with military glory. They were youths during the cynical twenties, and young men when the Depression brought poverty, unemployment, and the apparent collapse of capitalistic democracy. They were of military age during the years when fascism rose in Europe and the Second World War began to seem inevitable.

It is difficult, perhaps, for a younger generation, one that lives habitually with hydrogen bombs and accepts the constant presence of terror somewhere on the earth, to comprehend the shock of being young in the thirties. Orwell's generation was the first for whom world wars, dictators, Storm Troopers, concentration camps, mass unemployment, and poverty composed the realities of Europe. It was impossible to ignore those public, political realities, impossible to live the wholly private life or to play the role of the indifferent artist. All one could do, it seemed, was to face the world, to commit oneself, and to try to turn art into action.

Certainly it is to the credit of the young men of the thirties that they did commit themselves to action. But it was also, as Orwell recognized, their misfortune. For how was one to perform "the essentially public, non-individual activities" that the age required, and yet "love the surface of the earth"? How could the private and the public man be reconciled? Orwell struggled with this problem all his life and only solved it occasionally and imperfectly. He *was* an artist; he *did* care about style and the future of the English language; he took an artist's pleasure in the particularities of life—the earth, objects, and useless information. But he lived his creative life during the fourth and fifth decades of our century, and he accepted the pressures of the age. A poem that he wrote during the thirties begins, "A happy vicar I might have been/ Two hundred years ago." That vein of nostalgia for a simpler life in a simpler past was part of Orwell's nature, and it turns up in his novels; but he tried to suppress it, and faced instead the "evil time" to which he had been born.

To explain fully Orwell's qualities as a writer, one must go beyond the general history of his generation to his personal history. In Orwell's life before he became a writer there were three crucial, formative experiences. First, there was his experience of class. He was, as he put it with meticulous precision, a member of "the lower-upper-middle class," at the bottom, that is, of the class most concerned with position —being a gentleman, keeping up appearances, and preserving a sense of superiority. He went to Eton, but only because he won a scholarship, and he was miserably aware that he was among boys who were much richer than he was, and knew it. Snobbery and class remained important themes in his books.

When Orwell left Eton he joined the Indian Imperial Police and was sent to serve in Burma. There he had his second formative experience, the experience of oppression. He returned to England five years later a bitter anti-imperialist, filled with sympathy for the downtrodden and exploited. Those feelings are recorded in the writings that draw on the years in Burma: the novel *Burmese Days* and two autobiographical pieces, "A Hanging" and "Shooting an Elephant."

The third important experience was a consequence of the first two, and, it would seem, was consciously sought; it was the experience of poverty. After his return to England, Orwell set out to know and understand the poor by living among them. He went to Paris and lived in a working-class district for a time and earned his living as a dishwasher. Back in England, he lived in the poorest part of London, and sometimes traveled the roads of England with tramps and beggars. By the time this period ended Orwell knew more about the realities of poverty than any English writer since Dickens. "My theme is poverty" he wrote of his first book, and if poverty includes poverty of the spirit, it was always his theme.

Out of these experiences of class, oppression, and poverty Orwell evolved the deeply held personal values that give his life and writings the quality of moral integrity. His values were never, strictly speaking, political, though they were consistent with the emotional liberalism that Orwell professed, and called socialism. Most fundamentally, he believed in decency. This term implied both a kind of human behavior —decent treatment of one's fellow men preceded all reforms in Orwell's mind—and a recognition of basic human needs—men must have food, shelter, and a minimal amount of privacy before they can reach toward higher goals. From decency, liberty followed, for Orwell recognized that freedom depended on the achievement of a decent life. One of the principal themes in his books about poverty (*Down and Out in Paris and London* and *The Road to Wigan Pier*) is that no hungry man is ever free; to be poor is to be in chains.

After decency and liberty came justice, which is both a consequence and a foundation of decency; for decency depends on all men accepting every man's right to equal treatment before the law, but equality comes not from the law, but from the heart. Orwell said of Dickens that he believed that "If men would be decent, the world would be decent," and the same seems true of Orwell. But for Orwell, decency had political implications. The societies that he most admired—the coal miners of the English midlands and the loyalist troops in the Spanish Civil

War—were, as he saw them, communities of decent men, and the world of the future that filled him with such deep despair was a world in which decency would be forbidden.

In "Why I Write," Orwell said that "every line of serious work that I have written since 1936 has been written, directly or indirectly, *against* totalitarianism and *for* democratic Socialism, as I understand it." *(CEJL,* I, 5) The division that Orwell makes here in his career seems sharper than his books reveal, for everything he wrote was against oppression and for liberty, and in these general terms he was a consistently political writer all his life. But it is true that in his later books and essays the threat and the horror of a totalitarian future became an insistent, obsessive theme. The democratic socialism that he was for was always a good deal less explicit, but this is simply because Orwell's political convictions were never very precise, though they were deeply felt.

The turning point in 1936 was the beginning of the Spanish Civil War. The war had an immediate effect on British intellectuals, especially those of the Left; it made fascism seem a clear and present danger and the need for action urgent. Many Englishmen, including Orwell, went to Spain to fight for the Loyalists. He enlisted in the militia of the POUM (Partida Obrero de Unificación Marxista), an anti-Stalinist Marxist party, and was wounded in action. While he was recovering, the POUM was violently suppressed by the Stalinist-dominated Spanish government, and Orwell had to flee Spain to escape arrest. He returned to London and wrote *Homage to Catalonia* to tell the truth about the communist suppression of the non-Stalinist Left in Spain. It is the clearest example among Orwell's writings of a book that is directly against totalitarianism and for democratic socialism.

In Spain Orwell had firsthand experience of communism in action. Reports from Russia of Stalin's purge trials further convinced him that Soviet communism was a corruption of true socialism; like fascism, it denied the basic human values—decency, liberty, and justice—that Orwell believed in. For the rest of his life he attacked both communism and fascism as alternate forms of the political brutality that he hated and feared.

The victory of fascism in Spain, the growing power of Nazi Germany, and the failure of liberal democracies to oppose their enemies were profoundly discouraging to men like Orwell, who had hoped that free men might act to save themselves. As the Second World War approached, Orwell's vision of the future became more and more apocalyptic, more despairing, and less political in any positive sense. "Everyone with any imagination can foresee that Fascism . . . will be imposed on us as soon as the war starts," he wrote to a friend in September 1937; (*CEJL*, I, 284) and the following spring he remarked that "we might as well all pack our bags for the concentration camp." (*CEJL*, I, 309) In his last prewar novel, *Coming Up for Air*, he gave his ordinary, man-in-the-street protagonist this thought:

> War is coming. 1941, they say . . . *It's all going to happen.* All the things you've got at the back of your mind, the things you're terrified of, the things that you tell yourself are just a nightmare or only happen in foreign countries. The bombs, the food-queues, the rubber truncheons, the barbed wire, the coloured shirts, the slogans, the enormous faces, the machine-guns squirting out of bedroom windows. It's all going to happen. (*Coming Up for Air*, p. 274)

For Orwell, the coming of the war was not so much a new horror as a confirmation of the horror that he expected; it supported his conviction that the era of liberalism had come to an end. "Almost certainly," he wrote in 1940, "we are moving into an age of totalitarian dictatorships—an age in which freedom of thought will be at first a deadly sin and later on a meaningless abstraction." (*CEJL*, I, 525) Though he seemed, at least in his gloomier moments, to regard this approaching age as inevitable, he nevertheless behaved as though he felt both hope and patriotic instincts: he worked hard for his government during the war, largely as a writer for the BBC, and in his private writings he testified to "the spiritual need for patriotism and the military virtues." (*CEJL*, I, 540)

It was just after the war ended that Orwell achieved his first popular success with *Animal Farm*. By then his health, which had never been good and which had deteriorated during the hard war years, began to fail. He moved to an island in the Hebrides, and there, during 1946 and 1947, he wrote the first draft of *1984*. By the end of 1947 he was seriously ill with tuberculosis, but he continued to write, postponing medical treatment until he had finished revising the manuscript. He was in and out of hospitals during 1948 and 1949 and died in January 1950.

II

Serious writers put their own biographies into their books; whatever transformations the imagination may impose upon facts, what remains is the individual record of the life that mattered. Certainly this is true of Orwell. One can trace through his writing the course of his deepest concerns, the episodes that he felt to be significant, and his changing sense of the age. What one has in the end is both a life of George Orwell and a personal record of life in England in the 1930s and 40s.

I have mentioned three evils that dominated Orwell's mind—class, oppression, and poverty—and three values that he set against those evils—decency, liberty, and justice. Around these terms one could shape the whole story of Orwell's mind and art, taking the fiction and the nonfiction together as a whole. There is no book of Orwell's that is not about the poor: he was obsessed by what the lack of money does to the human spirit. There is no book that is not about class: one definition of poverty is having less than other members of your class, and Orwell, who had known this kind of poverty as a boy, returned in his fiction to the impoverished middle classes, and the spiritual expense of being genteel on too little income. There is no book that is not about oppression: for oppression follows naturally upon class and poverty. The oppressed may be Burmese (in *Burmese Days*), or French (*Down and Out in Paris and London*), or English (*A Clergyman's Daughter*), but the point is the same: so long as men have power over other men, so long as men can be divided into the rulers and the ruled, oppression will exist.

Orwell's sense of the evils of his age permeates his books, both the novels and the documentary studies. Nevertheless, the books differ in their impact, and most readers would agree that the fiction—at least up to *Animal Farm*—is inferior to the nonfiction. What the earlier novels lack is a sense of life, of characters who give their own momentum to their actions. This is paradoxical if one considers that these novels are more personal and autobiographical than the other books, and that the most autobiographical novel, *Keep the Aspidistra Flying*, is the weakest book Orwell wrote, but it is nevertheless true. When Orwell set about to turn the inner life into art, he did so without conviction, and the best parts of these novels are the least novelistic sections—those parts that are most nearly documentary.

One might say of these novels that they are weak because Orwell did not have a sufficiently high regard for the world of pure imagination. He respected the craft of writing and the medium of language, but he did not think of himself as a real novelist, and he was always willing to violate the imaginative unity of a novel to get things into it that he wanted to say. "One difficulty I have never solved," he wrote to his friend Julian Symons, "is that one has masses of experience which one passionately wants to write about . . . and no way of using them up except by disguising them as a novel." (*CEJL*, IV, 422) This is clearly the motive for many episodes in his novels—the hop-picking scenes in *A Clergyman's Daughter*, the jail scene in *Keep the Aspidistra Flying*, and the Left Book Club lecture in *Coming Up for Air*. All of these episodes are polemical (or as Orwell put it, examples of "the essentially public, non-individual activities that this age forces on all of us"); none is functional to the novel in which it appears.

Orwell could do such things to his own novels, I think, simply because they *were* fictions: his sense of human integrity, which was so strong in his own life, did not extend to imagined lives. When he talked about writing, he stressed his reverence for actuality—the surface of the earth, solid objects, scraps of useless information—but he did not seem to feel the same reverence for imagined worlds. In his best single piece of criticism, his long essay on Dickens, he says very little about Dickens as an artist: "I have been discussing Dickens simply in terms of his 'message,' " he writes toward the end of that essay, "and almost ignoring his literary qualities. But every writer, especially every novelist, *has* a 'message,' whether he admits it or not, and the minutest details of his work are influenced by it. All art is propaganda." (*CEJL*, I, 448) But, as he goes on to say, not all propaganda is art, and Orwell's early novels are flawed as novels by his willingness to allow the evidences of social evil to enter his fictive worlds too freely.

The same impulse can be seen at work in the nonfictional books— even in the best of them, *Homage to Catalonia*, which Orwell consciously weakened as a work of narrative art in order to insert material defending a political cause in Spain. The aesthetic instinct always gave way to the polemical on moral grounds: "I could not have done otherwise," he said of his writing of *Homage*. "I happened to know, what very few people in England had been allowed to know, that innocent men were being falsely accused. If I had not been angry about that I should never have written the book." (*CEJL*, I, 6) Orwell was always an angry writer—in the novels as much as elsewhere—and generally in good causes. But good anger does not make good art: the qualities that make *Homage to Catalonia* and *The Road to Wigan Pier* moving and strong weigh down the fiction.

Orwell was a middle-class, urban, South-of-England man, and his imagination worked best within those limits. In his novels he tried to expand the range of his imagination through documentary passages, but what is strictly imagined is a restricted segment of life. The principal characters are mostly from the sinking middle class, and there are no developed characters from the destitute poor (the most elaborate scene involving such people—the Trafalgar Square episode in *A Clergyman's Daughter*—is the most literary and derivative and the least successful in the novel), or from the upper classes (Ravelston in *Keep the Aspidistra Flying* is an improbable stock gentleman). The natural world, business, and domestic life are not given much attention. Most significantly perhaps, the real working classes—that is, urban industrial workers—never figure at all in the novels; Orwell could idealize, even sentimentalize the workers and the kind of socialism that he thought they represented, but he could not imagine them.

But the most serious limitation of the early novels, given Orwell's values and beliefs, is that none of them contains a hero: no one acts out the values of decency, liberty, and justice. Flory, Dorothy Hare, Gordon Comstock, and George Bowling are all weak people, tied by the conventions of their class and defeated by the impersonal forces of society. The lives we watch them living are empty, not only of positive public actions—the kind of gestures we might expect of a socialist novelist—but even of positive emotions; they have the lives, thoughts, and feelings appropriate to victims. In the world of the novels, decency always loses.

It is not really surprising, considering Orwell's reverence for actuality, that his imagination was freed, and his values realized, in his nonfictional books. By basing the writing on facts, Orwell verified and validated his motives, but he did not confine himself to the recording function of mere documentary: the books remain works of the imagination.

Orwell provides a striking example of the process by which documentation is transformed into imaginative reality in the use he makes, in *The Road to Wigan Pier,* of an episode that he first recorded in a diary entry made while he was researching the book. The diary reads:

> Passing up a horrible squalid side-alley, saw a woman, youngish but very pale and with the usual draggled exhausted look, kneeling by the gutter outside a house and poking a stick up the leaden waste-pipe, which was blocked. I thought how dreadful a destiny it was to be kneeling in the gutter in a back-alley in Wigan, in the bitter cold, prodding a stick up a blocked drain. At that moment she looked up and caught my eye, and her expression was as desolate as I have ever seen; it struck me that she was thinking just the same thing as I was. (*CEJL,* I, 177–78)

In *The Road to Wigan Pier,* the episode has been shaped and enriched, its significance heightened:

> The train bore me away, through the monstrous scenery of slag-heaps, chimneys, piled scrap-iron, foul canals, paths of cindery mud criss-crossed by the prints of clogs. This was March, but the weather had been horribly cold and everywhere there were mounds of blackened snow. As we moved slowly through the outskirts of the town we passed row after row of little grey slum houses running at right angles to the embankment. At the back of one of the houses a young woman was kneeling on the stones, poking a stick up the leaden waste-pipe which ran from the sink inside and which I suppose was blocked. I had time to see everything about her— her sacking apron, her clumsy clogs, her arms reddened by the cold. She

looked up as the train passed, and I was almost near enough to catch her eye. She had a round pale face, the usual exhausted face of the slum girl who is twenty-five and looks forty, thanks to miscarriages and drudgery; and it wore, for the second in which I saw it, the most desolate, hopeless expression I have ever seen. It struck me then that we are mistaken when we say that "It isn't the same for them as it would be for us," and that people bred in the slums can imagine nothing but the slums. For what I saw in her face was not the ignorant suffering of an animal. She knew well enough what was happening to her—understood as well as I did how dreadful a destiny it was to be kneeling there in the bitter cold, on the slimy stones of a slum backyard, poking a stick up a foul drain-pipe. (*Road*, p. 18)

All the best qualities of Orwell's mind are here: the particularity of his vision, the pity for poverty and suffering, the reverence for individual lives. The passage is polemical—it is against human misery and hopelessness—but it is not very precise propaganda. If we try to express its content in an imperative, we must reduce it to something like this: Feel pity! Though the example is generalized to stand for a class of wretched women, it never ceases to be particular—*this* poor woman, alone with her clogged drain and her destiny. What remains is a vividly experienced imaginative moment made out of an actual one.

The heroes who are missing from the novels appear in the documentary books— active, admired, sometimes larger than life. They are men like the coal miners in *The Road to Wigan Pier,* whose demonic underworld lives Orwell seems to envy even while he deplores their working conditions, the Spanish militiamen in *Homage to Catalonia,* and the shrewd, independent-minded tramps of *Down and Out in Paris and London.* Most of them are from the working class, but Orwell does not treat them as representatives of a class, in any strict political sense, but as possessors of a kind of natural energy that comes from sources outside man's social existence. They are Orwell's essential men, and they are the center of what hope he had for mankind. Their collective energies flow through these books and give them a vitality that the novels do not have.

III

"Books about ordinary people behaving in an ordinary manner are extremely rare," Orwell wrote in a review, "because they can only be written by some one who is capable of standing both inside and outside the ordinary man, as Joyce for instance stands inside and outside Bloom; but this involves admitting that you yourself *are* an ordinary person for nine-tenths of the time, which is exactly what no intellectual ever wants to do." The ostensible subject of this sentence was Henry

Miller's *Tropic of Cancer,* but the actual subject is clearly Orwell's own stance as a writer. Ordinariness as a measure of literary value occurs again and again in his critical writings, and so does its opposite, the intellectualism that he despised. In Orwell's own novels there are no exceptional people: no gifted artists, no beautiful women, no deep thinkers, no heroes, not even any exceptional villains.

Being ordinary was a virtue in fiction for Orwell because it was a virtue in life. "I have a sort of belly-to-earth attitude," he wrote to Miller, "and always feel uneasy when I get away from the ordinary world where grass is green, stones hard etc." He tried to live in that world himself; for a time he kept a country store and raised chickens and cabbages, and he seems to have made a point of looking and behaving like the most everyday sort of man. And the worlds that his imagination shaped are made of the same stuff: green grass, hard stones, and plain people. But when the imagination seizes such materials it may transform them, turn them into a myth of ordinariness that alters reality. For if being ordinary is a value, then the persons who embody that quality are elevated by it, and stand not as mere people but as representatives of value.

Orwell mythologized his idea of ordinariness in two related ways: in a Myth of the Proletariat (where ordinariness was given a class identity), and in a Myth of the English People (where it was made a national characteristic). The Proletariat Myth is developed most fully in *The Road to Wigan Pier,* where the working class is described as stronger, happier, more honest, and—in its working-class way—wiser than the middle class, and particularly superior to the intellectuals. Here is a typical passage:

> I have often been struck by the peculiar easy completeness, the perfect symmetry as it were, of a working-class interior at its best. Especially on winter evenings after tea, when the fire glows in the open range and dances mirrored in the steel fender, when Father, in shirt-sleeves, sits in the rocking chair at one side of the fire reading the racing finals, and Mother sits on the other with her sewing, and the children are happy with a pennorth of mint humbugs, and the dog lolls roasting himself on the rag mat—it is a good place to be in, provided that you can be not only in it but sufficiently *of* it to be taken for granted. (*Road to Wigan Pier,* p. 149)

In a book concerned with unemployment and poverty among the industrial workers, this idyllic Dickensian scene strikes an odd note, but for Orwell it was a vision of ideal human felicity, and he regretted that in the "utopian future" it would necessarily disappear. It is also an *exclusive* scene, open only to workers who belong (and Orwell with his Etonian accent and his art never could); it is private and domestic, not social or political. Its political implications, insofar as it has any, are conservative.

Orwell's mythical proletarian may be a socialist, and it is reasonable that he should be, but in his own way. "So far as my experience goes," Orwell observed, "no genuine working man grasps the deeper implications of Socialism. Often, in my opinion, he is a truer Socialist than the orthodox Marxist, because he does remember, what the other often forgets, that Socialism means justice and common decency." (*Road*, p. 208; see also *CEJL*, I, 335–36) This comes close to the weak-mind-but-strong-heart view of the working class, a view that is both patronizing and sentimental. It is nevertheless a part of Orwell's myth.

Orwell's workers are also, of course, English, and his Myth of the English People shares some of the qualities that he found in English working men. His Englishman is phlegmatic, patriotic, decent, law-abiding; he is also insensitive to art, hostile to abstraction, and incapable of logical thought. He is, as Orwell describes him at length in *The English People*, the apotheosis of ordinariness. He appears in various forms in the English characters of *Burmese Days*, in George Bowling of *Coming Up for Air*, and in many minor characters of the early books. (Most of Orwell's tramps are examples of essential English qualities.) He also appears in the role that Orwell chose to play in his own life— the simple, decent chap who hates cities and intellectuals and simply has to have "a bit of garden and a few animals."

Orwell's imagination was ordinary and English (in his sense of those terms) chiefly in its reverence for what was physical, factual, and particular. He thought it important for a novelist to know about "how things really happen," and his books instruct us in the particulars of many crafts and skills—how to be a pavement artist, how to pick hops, how to beg, how to mine coal, how to be a dishwasher. Some of these are from the documentary books, but others are from the novels; there is little distinction to be made in the degree of particularity involved. Even the most general passages of a book ostensibly devoted to a general subject, like *The Road to Wigan Pier*, are full of anecdotes, examples, and facts—things that an ordinary man might know. It is perhaps a part of Orwell's Englishness that he disliked abstractions and distrusted intellectuals; he was not, strictly speaking, anti-intellectual, but he was hostile toward the kind of middle-class people who classify themselves as intellectuals rather than as ordinary men. He believed that truth was to be found, not on the level of abstractions, but on the surface of the earth.

If Orwell's imagination was particular, it was also puritanical; he avoided pleasure as a subject in much the same way that he avoided abstractions, and perhaps for a similar reason—pleasure was fanciful, and raised above the earth-bound realities of poverty and pain. He criticized Arthur Koestler for his "well-marked hedonistic strain," (*CEJL,* III, 244) and his own works showed the opposite impulse—toward self-abnegation, ugliness, and the physically disgusting. Orwell's most memorable scenes are scenes of human degradation, humiliation, and defeat: the Paris scullery in *Down and Out,* the slum lodging house in *Wigan Pier,* Flory's suicide, and the whole episode of "Shooting an Elephant." The books give us almost no sense that he had ever experienced the common human happinesses: consider, for example, his treatment of marriage, sexual love, children, food and drink, friendship, and natural landscape. The world that his imagination could credit and create was one in which men are victims; he did not allow himself the indulgence of joy.

Orwell defended his choice of subjects by arguing his political purposes and the inevitability of politics. "In our age," he wrote, "there is no such thing as 'keeping out of politics.' All issues are political issues. . . ." (*CEJL,* IV, 137) This was Orwell's way of affirming the moral value of his work; but to make such a statement is surely to confess a limitation and to reveal an obsession. Orwell was willing to violate the form of his work to make a political point, but he was unwilling (or perhaps unable) to modify the relentless impoverishment of life that was his subject, to allow that even in our age there are private values that cannot be turned into political issues but that, nevertheless, exist to nourish and sustain us.

IV

Though Orwell believed that all art is propaganda and no book is free of political bias, he aspired to make his political writing into art. "Why I Write" is a self-conscious attempt to reconcile political motives and aesthetic achievement, and in many other essays he testified to his concern for style and the nurture of the English language. One can see, in these various remarks, how Orwell's convictions about men and politics led to ideas about the use of words; not only his art, but his ideas about art, had political bases.

One might readily infer what those ideas are by considering Orwell's two myths. The Myth of the Proletariat leads to the assertion that "language ought to be the joint creation of poets and manual workers" (*English People,* p. 39) and to the belief that when the educated classes lose touch with the workers, the language suffers. The result is a theory of plain style, which Orwell summarized in this way:

> To write or even to speak English is not a science but an art. There are no reliable rules: there is only the general principle that concrete words

are better than abstract ones, and that the shortest way of saying anything is always the best. (*English People*, p. 33)

By these principles Shakespeare and Milton, and indeed most English poets, would stand condemned; but the prose writers whom Orwell admired most—Swift and Dickens—would be approved. Not only in his principles but also in his dismissal of the very idea of rules, Orwell assumed an ordinary man's attitude: short and simple is the best, plain talk is the honest way for plain people.

Orwell developed his Myth of Englishness in relation to language most elaborately and lovingly in *The English People*, though it is implicit in all his writings on style. What he liked about his own language was its range of tone, its grammatical simplicity, its large vocabulary, and its adaptability. But he worried that it was being debased by jargon and American borrowings, and was losing contact with its native roots. In this essay the language almost assumes the character of a simple, honest Englishman exposed to temptations from the world. Orwell's general attitude is conservative, taking the language of the past as the ideal and urging a purer and more English usage.

Orwell's ideas of style had political sources, and he saw a close connection between language and politics. Political corruption corrupted language; but also "the slovenliness of our language makes it easier for us to have foolish thoughts." (*CEJL*, IV, 128) The use of language is therefore both a political and a moral act. In his essay "Politics and the English Language," Orwell cites several examples of bad usage that are all bad in the same way—they have lost concreteness, freshness, and precision, and have become vague and abstract. Orwell says that these weaknesses are particularly common in political writing, by which he means *bad* political writing. The opposite style would be one of careful ordinariness and particularity—the style of Orwell's best work, and the style of common speech.

When Orwell praised another writer, it was usually for his concreteness. In Dickens, for instance, he admired the unnecessary detail that made a comic narrative vividly actual, and he tried for the same sort of effect in his own work. For example, this description of a lodging house kitchen table:

> I never saw this table completely uncovered, but I saw its various wrappings at different times. At the bottom there was a layer of old newspapers stained by Worcester Sauce; above that a sheet of sticky white oilcloth; above that a green serge cloth; above that a coarse linen cloth, never changed and seldom taken off. Generally the crumbs from breakfast were still on the table at supper. I used to get to know individual crumbs by sight and watch their progress up and down the table from day to day. (*Road to Wigan Pier*, p. 7)

The Dickensian detail is the migratory crumbs. But the whole passage is a model of the kind of language that Orwell trusted—plain, particular, and English. It is true to the world of Orwell's imagination: it is concerned with the exact description of impoverishment, but it also manages to give one the feeling of being poor. It gets its effects by naming, not by abstracting; it is the language of the surface of the earth.

Orwell believed that "the present political chaos is connected with the decay of language, and that one can probably bring about some improvement by starting at the verbal end." (*CEJL*, IV, 139) His own efforts to achieve that improvement are evident in his essays on language, in his own careful style, and most elaborately in the principles of "Newspeak" in *1984*. It was at this point, on the morality of language, that Orwell the artist and Orwell the polemicist were most nearly one.

V

1984 was Orwell's last novel, and it seems as one reads it, that he must have written it with the knowledge that he might not write another. It would be melodramatic to say that he knew he was dying, but certainly he knew that he was seriously ill. The writing was a slow and difficult process, broken by periods when he was too weak to work. *Burmese Days* took him a year to write, and *A Clergyman's Daughter* was finished in about ten months, but the writing of *1984* stretched over more than two years. In the end he thought that his illness had gotten into the book and had spoiled it. Nevertheless, it is his best book, the one in which he most successfully turned his values and beliefs, the things he cherished and the things he feared and hated, into a form of fiction. More than any of his other books, *1984* contains a complete, imagined world, a political nightmare made actual and ordinary.

While he was writing the book Orwell described it, in a letter to his publisher, as "a novel about the future—that is, it is in a sense a fantasy, but in the form of a naturalistic novel." This remark points obliquely to an essential quality in the book, its ambiguous relation to future and present time. Though it is set in the future, it is not "futuristic"; the evolution of modern science held none of the fascination for Orwell that it did for H. G. Wells, and his world-of-the-future has no scientific wonders in it—no flying machines, or super-weapons, or space technology to separate it from our own experience. His characters walk the streets of a London that is very like the London of World War II. Joy has been subtracted from their world, but nothing has been added.

Orwell also called his book "a Utopia in the form of a novel." This seems an odd description—we usually think of utopias as imagined ideal societies—but Orwell's point is that his novel is to be read as a warning, not as a prophecy. Utopias do not predict the future; they judge the present. The best modern examples of the genre of *1984*— H. G. Wells' *Time Machine*, Huxley's *Brave New World*, Golding's *Lord of the Flies*—use future time in similar ways, to isolate and emphasize certain aspects of the human situation in order to focus attention on them; the intention is admonitory, not prophetic. Orwell was pointing to the same qualities in his book, when he noted the elements of parody and satire in it.

In obvious ways, *1984* is a product of the postwar years. In those years England's socialist government, facing shortages of money, housing, and even food, had imposed on the people a life more austere and controlled than the war years had been. And in Europe the iron curtain had come down, dividing the communist world from the west on a scale that Orwell had predicted and feared. Both the austerity and the international division of the world enter the novel in important ways.

But for the real beginnings of *1984* we must go back a good deal farther to Orwell's experiences in the thirties. Then, as he saw totalitarianism spreading over Europe, he began to imagine that it might also come to England. The imagining was at first very vague, no more precise than fear itself: "Presently there may be coming God knows what horrors," he wrote in *The Road to Wigan Pier*, "horrors of which, in this sheltered island, we have not even a traditional knowledge." But history gave the horror particularity, and by the end of *Coming Up for Air*, George Bowling can imagine the approaching war in details that become part of the symbolic texture of *1984*: the rubber truncheons, the slogans, the enormous faces. This book was written early in 1939, and one might say that by this point the world of *1984* had become alive in Orwell's imagination.

At about the same time Orwell was thinking about the immediate future in other ways that anticipated his last novel. "It is quite possible," he wrote in January 1939, "that we are descending into an age in which two and two will make five when the Leader says so" (*CEJL*, I, 376), and the following year he wrote this passage on totalitarian "thought control":

It not only forbids you to express—even to think—certain thoughts, but it dictates what you *shall* think, it creates an ideology for you, it tries to govern your emotional life as well as setting up a code of conduct. And as far as possible it isolates you from the outside world, it shuts you up in an artificial universe in which you have no standards of comparison. The totalitarian state tries, at any rate, to control the thoughts and emotions

of its subjects at least as completely as it controls their actions. (*CEJL,*
II, 135)

Here the novel's central theme—the imposition of the state's will upon
thought and truth—is explicit. But theme depends on particulars, and
it is interesting to note, looking back over these beginnings, how early
Orwell had hit upon symbolic expressions of totalitarian control—the
enormous faces, the arithmetical lie, the Leader. These are symbols
that carry the emotional force of the political ideas they express; they
make the novel, the act of political imagination, possible.

It is well, though, when we begin to consider *1984* as a political
novel, to go back to "Why I Write," and to remind ourselves of the
tension that Orwell felt between the public and the private lives. For
that tension is at the heart of the novel. When Winston Smith thinks,
"Nothing was your own except the few cubic centimeters inside your
skull," he is expressing the base on which Orwell's whole morality
rests: to be human is to be private, to have a personal identity that is
inward and inviolable. Smith's rebellion against authority is an attempt to preserve that small circle of privacy: to think, to feel, and to
believe as himself. Authority tries to destroy personal identity entirely,
by any means; significantly, the only sciences in which the world of
1984 is in advance of the present are the science of invading privacy
and the science of torture, two ways of controlling and altering identity.

Starting from the proposition that personal identity is fixed and private, one can go on to other propositions: that the past is unchange-
able, that truth is objective, that words have fixed meanings. And that
love is possible. Taken together these propositions define a relationship
to reality that we take for granted; *1984* is horrible because in it every
one of these propositions is denied. These ideas have been fundamental to western, liberal culture since the Renaissance; our institutions, our sciences, our humane studies, our arts, our human relationships all depend on them. But as Orwell makes clear, they are all
luxuries: man can live without a past, without truth, without clear
language, and even without love. But though man can survive, his
humanity and his civilization cannot. It is partly the sense of the end
of a great, liberating period of human culture, the sense that the Renaissance has ended, that makes the novel so profoundly depressing. It's
not simply that language and love do not exist in Oceania; it's that
they *did* exist, but have been destroyed.

The values of the novel, then, are political values, and Orwell's
reverence for them places him in a political tradition—the central liberal tradition of western culture. But they do not imply specific political action, or a party, or a system. Here, as in his earlier books, Orwell's
politics amount to decency, liberty, and justice; if men would be de-

cent, the world would be decent. And, as in the other books, ordinariness is a source of value. Orwell had chosen, as he said, "the form of a naturalistic novel," in order that the action might be rooted in a setting of gritty, everyday reality, and he invented as his protagonist a man without exceptional qualities, so that the whole novel is filled with a sense of probable, typical existence. Thus, Smith's need for truth and love are *ordinary* needs, such as we might feel under a totalitarian system, and his hope is in ordinary people. Smith shares Orwell's belief in the Myth of the Proletariat, as we see when he seeks out the old man in the pub to discover the truth about the past, and when, looking at the washerwoman, he thinks that "the proles are immortal." This, too, is a political statement, but it scarcely amounts to socialism: it is simply a faith in the survival of ordinary people, beyond systems. The action of the novel does nothing to confirm this faith; it simply exists as faith, as it did in Orwell's mind.

I have said before that Orwell's imagination was one that depended upon documentation and the sense of recorded fact. This quality of mind is very evident in *1984,* and it creates some formal problems. It is most obviously evident in the close connection between certain figures in the novel and their historical counterparts. Big Brother looks like Stalin, Goldstein is a Trotsky-like dissenting intellectual, and the purges, trials, and tortures resemble those that decimated the Russian party during the thirties. A reader with a reasonable knowledge of modern history may think that he is reading a fictionalized commentary on actual political events, which is therefore a less than fully imagined work of fiction. But what Orwell did was to take figures and episodes that had already become mythical (no one knew, for example, the truth about the purges or Trotsky's role in the alleged plot against Stalin), and make his own myth out of them. Being political and historical, they were available to Orwell's peculiar documenting imagination; being mythical, they could be assimilated into art.

There is another kind of documentation in the novel that raises a different problem. A footnote on the third page refers to "Newspeak" and adds: "For an account of its structure and etymology, see Appendix." If one turns to the appendix, one finds a fourteen-page essay titled "The Principles of Newspeak," in which the new language of Oceania is treated as a reality. Furthermore, in the center of the book the action stops altogether while Smith reads long extracts from *The Theory and Practice of Oligarchical Collectivism,* by Emmanuel Goldstein, a work that sounds like a genuine political polemic. Both of these documents are invented and are as much products of Orwell's imagination as any episode in the narrative. But their function in the novel is different; they are there as a kind of make-believe documenta-

tion, to give the world of the novel the same sort of validation that
interviews and statistical tables give to *The Road to Wigan Pier*. They
make that world more horrible by verifying it. Both are, in their ways,
political documents—Goldstein's book obviously and directly, "Newspeak" through Orwell's conviction that there is a reciprocal relation
between politics and language—and they expand the political substance of the book beyond conventional limits. Neither is a flaw, given
the peculiar nature of the novel.

In the 'end of *1984*, Winston Smith and personal values have lost,
and one is left, it seems, with an unqualified pessimism; O'Brien calls
Smith "the last man," and the last man has been deprived of his
identity, and loves Big Brother. The novel concludes, then, that the
complete destruction of the human spirit is possible. But to read this as
a surrender to the reality of power is an error; one can only do so by
reading the naturalistic novel and ignoring the fantasy. For *1984* is a
satire and a warning, not a description; men have created political institutions in this century that could destroy all decency, liberty, and
justice, and indeed over large areas of the earth this has already happened. But the last man has not lost yet, and the human ideals that
Orwell believed in and put into his novel are still possible. We have
only to protect and value them enough to keep them alive.

"England is lacking," Orwell wrote during the war, "in what one
might call concentration-camp literature. The special world created by
secret-police forces, censorship of opinion, torture and frame-up trials
is, of course, known about and to some extent disapproved of, but it
has made very little emotional impact. . . . To understand such
things one has to be able to imagine oneself as the victim." Orwell had
that quality of imagination: all his main characters are victims, and he
saw the political world as an essentially victimizing one. And so he was
able to give England the concentration-camp literature that it lacked.
But he did so that men might not be victims, that the "special world"
of totalitarianism might be kept from his own country.

VI

Perhaps every age needs its own nightmare, and *1984* is ours. It is
a nightmare peculiar to our time, for only in this century has totalitarianism become an actuality, and thus a subject for the human imagination: only where there *were* boots in human faces, could one imagine
a boot stamping on a human face—forever.

But if Orwell offers us nightmare, he also offers daylight sanity of a
very simple kind. There is a passage in *The English People* in which
Orwell asks himself whether national cultures exist, and concludes

that "this is one of those questions, like the freedom of the will or the identity of the individual, in which all the arguments are on one side and instinctive knowledge is on the other." On these questions, Orwell is always on the side of instinctive knowledge; he believed in the authority of the human heart. The things he valued—privacy, decency, the human spirit—rise from sources deeper than philosophy or logic. Winston Smith's beliefs are as simple as two plus two equal four: the past is fixed, love is private, and the truth is beyond change. All have this in common: they set limits to men's power; they testify to the fact that some things cannot be changed. The point is beyond politics—it is a point of essential humanity.

V. S. Pritchett: *1984*

Nineteen Eighty-Four is a book that goes through the reader like an east wind, cracking the skin, opening the sores; hope has died in Mr. Orwell's wintry mind, and only pain is known. I do not think I have ever read a novel more frightening and depressing; and yet, such are the originality, the suspense, the speed of writing and withering indignation that it is impossible to put the book down. The faults of Orwell as a writer—monotony, nagging, the lonely schoolboy shambling down the one dispiriting track—are transformed now he rises to a large subject. He is the most devastating pamphleteer alive because he is the plainest and most individual—there is none of Koestler's lurid journalism—and because, with steady misanthropy, he knows exactly where on the new Jesuitism to apply the Protestant whip.

The story is simple. In 1984 Winston Smith, a civil servant and Party member in the English Totalitarian State (now known as Air Strip No. 1), conceives political doubts, drifts into tacit rebellion, is detected after a short and touching period of happiness with a girl member of the Party and is horribly "rehabilitated." Henceforth he will be spiritually, emotionally, intellectually infantile, passive and obedient, as though he had undergone a spiritual leucotomy. He is "saved" for the life not worth living. In *Darkness at Noon,* death was the eventual punishment of deviation: in 1984 the punishment is lifeless life.

> Oh, stubborn self-willed exile from the loving breast! Two gin-scented tears trickled down the sides of his nose. But it was all right, everything was all right, the struggle was finished. He had won the victory over himself. He loved Big Brother.

A generation from now the world is composed of three States, Oceania, Eurasia, Eastasia in perpetual war. From time to time these States change sides, and the mass of people have little clear idea at any moment of who are their allies or their enemies. These wars are mainly fought on the frontiers away from the great cities—for atom bombing turned out to be too destructive and made useful war impossible—and

"*1984*" by V. S. Pritchett. From The New Statesman and Nation *37, n.s. (June 18, 1949), 646–48. Reprinted by permission of the publisher.*

their objects are, fundamentally, to use up the excessive productiveness of the machine, and yet, contradictorily, to get control of rare raw materials or cheap native labour. Another important attraction of war is that it enables the new governing class, who are modelled on the Stalinists, to keep down the standard of living and nullify the intelligence of the masses who they no longer pretend to have liberated. War is peace: the party slogan indicates that war is not itself necessary; but that the collective oligarchy can operate securely only on a war footing.

It is with this moral corruption of absolute political power that Mr. Orwell's novel is concerned. London lies decaying like an old cabbage in the remains of its seedy 19th-century building, but high above the streets tower the four main ministries of Ingsoc: the Ministry of Truth, for the issuing of lies, that is to say, official news, official culture; the Ministry of Plenty, for the purpose of organising scarcity; the Ministry of Peace for conducting war; and the dubious Ministry of Love, windowless and surrounded by barbed wire and machine guns, where political prisoners are either executed or "rehabilitated" by the new Inquisition. A recalcitrant will enter the Ministry of Love and emerge eventually an official sponge, incapable of private life, without memory; private memory and the sexual impulse are the two deadly sins. Enjoying them, the virtues of obedience and hysteria are impossible to the citizen. In the homes of Party members—and all except the "proles" or workers have some place in this hierarchy—a telescreen is fitted, from which canned propaganda continually pours, on which the pictures of Big Brother, the leader and the ancient enemy and anti-Christ, Goldstein often appear. Also by this device the Thought Police, on endless watch for Thought Crime, can observe the people night and day. What precisely Thought Crime really is no one knows; but in general it is the tendency to conceive a private life secret from the State. A frown, a smile, a shadow on the face, a sigh may betray the citizen, who has forgotten, for the moment, the art of "reality control" or, in Newspeak, the official language, "doublethink." Winston Smith's doubts began when, accidentally, there came into his hands a complete piece of evidence of State lying. The doubts drove him to action: he bought a notebook and started a diary, that is to say, a piece of writing not directed by the State. He tried to define "doublethink":

> To know and not to know, to be conscious of complete truthfulness while telling carefully constructed lies, to hold simultaneously two opinions which cancelled out, knowing them to be contradictory and believing in both of them; to use logic against logic, to repudiate morality while laying claim to it, to believe that democracy was impossible and that the Party was the guardian of democracy; to forget whatever it was necessary to forget, then to draw it back into memory again at the mo-

ment it was needed, and then promptly to forget again; and, above all, to apply the same process to the process itself. That was the ultimate subtlety; consciously to induce unconsciousness, and then, once again, to become unconscious of the act of hypnosis you had just performed. Even to understand the word "doublethink" involved the use of double-think.

Newspeak, the new Basic English blessed by the scientists and the Party, is the natural offspring of Doublethink. "You think, I dare say," says Syme, the Party philologist, "that our chief job is inventing new words. But not a bit of it! We're destroying words, scores of them." And he goes on to give examples:

> It is a beautiful thing, the destruction of words. Of course, the great wastage is in the verbs and adjectives, but there are hundreds of nouns that can be got rid of as well. It isn't only the synonyms; there are also the antonyms. After all, what justification is there for a word which is simply the opposite of some other word? A word contains its opposite in itself. Take "good," for instance. If you have a word like "good," what need is there for a word like "bad." "Ungood" will do just as well— better, because it is the exact opposite which the other is not. Or, again, if you want a stronger version of "good," what sense is there in having a whole string of vague, useless words like "excellent" and "splendid" and all the rest of them. "Plusgood" covers the meaning.

The aim of Newspeak is to narrow the range of thought, and to remove from the classics all the subversiveness which could pollute the minds of Party Members. The time will come when the official slogans: War is Peace, Freedom is Slavery, Ignorance is Strength, will not be required, "simply because there will be no thought as we understand it now."

Mr. Orwell's book is a satirical pamphlet. I notice that some critics have said that his prophecy is not probable. Neither was Swift's *Modest Proposal* nor Wells's *Island of Dr. Moreau*. Probability is not a necessary condition of satire which, when it pretends to draw the future, is, in fact, scourging the present. The purges in Russia and, later, in the Russian satellites, the dreary seediness of London in the worst days of the war, the pockets of 19th-century life in decaying England, the sordidness of bad flats, bad food, the native and whining streak of domestic sluttishness which have sickened English satirists since Smollett, all these have given Mr. Orwell his material. The duty of the satirist is to go one worse than reality; and it might be objected that Mr. Orwell is too literal, that he is too oppressed by what he sees, to exceed it. In one or two incidents where he does exceed, notably in the torture scenes, he is merely melodramatic: he introduces those rather grotesque machines which used to appear in terror stories for boys. In one place

—I mean the moment when Winston's Inquisitor drives him to call out for the death of his girl, by threatening to set a cageful of famished rats on him—we reach a peak of imaginative excess in terror, but it is superfluous because mental terrorism is his real subject.

Until our time, irony and unnatural laughter were thought to be the duty of the satirist: in *Candide* the more atrocious the fact—and a large number of Voltaire's facts were true—the gayer the laugh. More strikingly than in any other genre, it is indispensable for satire to sound "untrue," an effect Voltaire obtained by running a large number of true things together in a natural manner. The laughter of Voltaire, the hatred of Swift were assertions of vitality and the instinct to live in us, which continually struggles not only against evil but against the daily environment.

But disgust, the power to make pain sickening, the taste for punishment, exceed irony and laughter in the modern satirist. Neither Winston Smith nor the author laughs when he discovers that the women of the new State are practised hypocrites and make fools of the Party members. For Mr. Orwell, the most honest writer alive, hypocrisy is too dreadful for laughter: it feeds his despair.

As a pamphleteer Orwell may be right in his choice of means. The life-instinct rebels against the grey tyrannies that, like the Jehovah of the Old Testament, can rule only as long as they create guilt. The heart sinks, but the spirit rebels as one reads Mr. Orwell's ruthless opening page, even though we have met that boiled cabbage in all his books before:

> It was a bright, cold day in April, and the clocks were striking thirteen. Winston Smith, his chin nuzzled into his breast in an effort to escape the vile wind, slipped quickly through the glass doors of Victory Mansions, though not quickly enough to prevent a swirl of gritty dust from entering along with him.
>
> The hallway smelt of boiled cabbage and old rag mats. . . . It was no use trying the lift. Even at the best of times it was seldom working, and at present the electricity current was cut off during daylight hours. It was part of the economy drive in preparation for Hate Week. The flat was seven flights up, and Winston, who was 39 and had a varicose ulcer above his right ankle, went slowly, resting several times on the way. On each landing, opposite the lift shaft, the poster with the enormous face gazed from the wall. It was one of those pictures which are so contrived that the eyes follow you about when you move. Big Brother IS WATCHING YOU, the caption beneath it ran.

But though the indignation of *Nineteen Eighty-Four* is singeing, the book does suffer from a division of purpose. Is it an account of present hysteria, is it a satire on propaganda, or a world that sees itself entirely in inhuman terms? Is Mr. Orwell saying, not that there is no hope, but that there is no hope for man in the political conception of man? We have come to the end of a movement. He is like some dour Protestant or Jansenist who sees his faith corrupted by the "doublethink" of the Roman Catholic Church, and who fiercely rejects the corrupt civilisations that appear to be able to flourish even under that dispensation.

Lionel Trilling: Orwell on the Future

George Orwell's new novel, "Nineteen Eighty-Four" (Harcourt, Brace), confirms its author in the special, honorable place he holds in our intellectual life. Orwell's native gifts are perhaps not of a transcendent kind; they have their roots in a quality of mind that ought to be as frequent as it is modest. This quality may be described as a sort of moral centrality, a directness of relation to moral—and political—fact, and it is so far from being frequent in our time that Orwell's possession of it seems nearly unique. Orwell is an intellectual to his fingertips, but he is far removed from both the Continental and the American type of intellectual. The turn of his mind is what used to be thought of as peculiarly "English." He is indifferent to the allurements of elaborate theory and of extreme sensibility. The medium of his thought is common sense, and his commitment to intellect is fortified by an old-fashioned faith that the truth can be got at, that we can, if we actually want to, see the object as it really is. This faith in the power of mind rests in part on Orwell's willingness, rare among contemporary intellectuals, to admit his connection with his own cultural past. He no longer identifies himself with the British upper middle class in which he was reared, yet it is interesting to see how often his sense of fact derives from some ideal of that class, how he finds his way through a problem by means of an unabashed certainty of the worth of some old, simple, belittled virtue. Fairness, decency, and responsibility do not make up a shining or comprehensive morality, but in a disordered world they serve Orwell as an invaluable base of intellectual operations.

Radical in his politics and in his artistic tastes, Orwell is wholly free of the cant of radicalism. His criticism of the old order is cogent, but he is chiefly notable for his flexible and modulated examination of

"*Orwell on the Future*" by Lionel Trilling. From The New Yorker, *June 18, 1949,* pp. 74–77. Copyright 1949 by The New Yorker Magazine, Inc. Reprinted by permission of the publisher.

the political and aesthetic ideas that oppose those of the old order. Two years of service in the Spanish Loyalist Army convinced him that he must reject the line of the Communist Party and, presumably, gave him a large portion of his knowledge of the nature of human freedom. He did not become—as Leftist opponents of Communism are so often and so comfortably said to become—"embittered" or "cynical"; his passion for freedom simply took account of yet another of freedom's enemies, and his intellectual verve was the more stimulated by what he had learned of the ambiguous nature of the newly identified foe, which so perplexingly uses the language and theory of light for ends that are not enlightened. His distinctive work as a radical intellectual became the criticism of liberal and radical thought wherever it deteriorated to shibboleth and dogma. No one knows better than he how willing is the intellectual Left to enter the prison of its own mass mind, nor does anyone believe more directly than he in the practical consequences of thought, or understand more clearly the enormous power, for good or bad, that ideology exerts in an unstable world.

"Nineteen Eighty-Four" is a profound, terrifying, and wholly fascinating book. It is a fantasy of the political future, and, like any such fantasy, serves its author as a magnifying device for an examination of the present. Despite the impression it may give at first, it is not an attack on the Labour Government. The shabby London of the Super-State of the future, the bad food, the dull clothing, the fusty housing, the infinite ennui—all these certainly reflect the English life of today, but they are not meant to represent the outcome of the utopian pretensions of Labourism or of any socialism. Indeed, it is exactly one of the cruel essential points of the book that utopianism is no longer a living issue. For Orwell, the day has gone by when we could afford the luxury of making our flesh creep with the spiritual horrors of a successful hedonistic society; grim years have intervened since Aldous Huxley, in "Brave New World," rigged out the welfare state of Ivan Karamazov's Grand Inquisitor in the knickknacks of modern science and amusement, and said what Dostoevski and all the other critics of the utopian ideal had said before—that men might actually gain a life of security, adjustment, and fun, but only at the cost of their spiritual freedom, which is to say, of their humanity. Orwell agrees that the State of the future will establish its power by destroying souls. But he believes that men will be coerced, not cosseted, into soullessness. They will be dehumanized not by sex, massage, and private helicopters but by a marginal life of deprivation, dullness, and fear of pain.

This, in fact, is the very center of Orwell's vision of the future. In 1984, nationalism as we know it has at last been overcome, and the world is organized into three great political entities. All profess the same philosophy, yet despite their agreement, or because of it, the three Super-States are always at war with each other, two always allied against one, but all seeing to it that the balance of power is kept, by means of sudden, treacherous shifts of alliance. This arrangement is established as if by the understanding of all, for although it is the ultimate aim of each to dominate the world, the immediate aim is the perpetuation of war without victory and without defeat. It has at last been truly understood that war is the health of the State; as an official slogan has it, "War Is Peace." Perpetual war is the best assurance of perpetual absolute rule. It is also the most efficient method of consuming the production of the factories on which the economy of the State is based. The only alternative method is to distribute the goods among the population. But this has its clear danger. The life of pleasure is inimical to the health of the State. It stimulates the senses and thus encourages the illusion of individuality; it creates personal desires, thus potential personal thought and action.

But the life of pleasure has another, and even more significant, disadvantage in the political future that Orwell projects from his observation of certain developments of political practice in the last two decades. The rulers he envisages are men who, in seizing rule, have grasped the innermost principles of power. All other oligarchs have included some general good in their impulse to rule and have played at being philosopher-kings or priest-kings or scientist-kings, with an announced program of beneficence. The rulers of Orwell's State know that power in its pure form has for its true end nothing but itself, and they know that the nature of power is defined by the pain it can inflict on others. They know, too, that just as wealth exists only in relation to the poverty of others, so power in its pure aspect exists only in relation to the weakness of others, and that any power of the ruled, even the power to experience happiness, is by that much a diminution of the power of the rulers.

The exposition of the *mystique* of power is the heart and essence of Orwell's book. It is implicit throughout the narrative, explicit in excerpts from the remarkable "Theory and Practice of Oligarchical Collectivism," a subversive work by one Emmanuel Goldstein, formerly the most gifted leader of the Party, now the legendary foe of the State. It is brought to a climax in the last section of the novel, in the terrible scenes in which Winston Smith, the sad hero of the story, having lost his hold on the reality decreed by the State, having come to believe that sexuality is a pleasure, that personal loyalty is good, and that two plus two always and not merely under certain circumstances equals four, is brought back to health by torture and discourse in a hideous parody on psychotherapy and the Platonic dialogues.

Orwell's theory of power is developed brilliantly, at considerable length. And the social system that it postulates is described with magnificent circumstantiality: the three orders of the population—Inner Party, Outer Party, and proletarians; the complete surveillance of the citizenry by the Thought Police, the only really efficient arm of the government; the total negation of the personal life; the directed emotions of hatred and patriotism; the deified Leader, omnipresent but invisible, wonderfully named Big Brother; the children who spy on their parents; and the total destruction of culture. Orwell is particularly successful in his exposition of the official mode of thought, Doublethink, which gives one "the power of holding two contradictory beliefs in one's mind simultaneously, and accepting both of them." This intellectual safeguard of the State is reinforced by a language, Newspeak, the goal of which is to purge itself of all words in which a free thought might be formulated. The systematic obliteration of the past further protects the citizen from Crimethink, and nothing could be more touching, or more suggestive of what history means to the mind, than the efforts of poor Winston Smith to think about the condition of man without knowledge of what others have thought before him.

By now, it must be clear that "Nineteen Eighty-Four" is, in large part, an attack on Soviet Communism. Yet to read it as this and as nothing else would be to misunderstand the book's aim. The settled and reasoned opposition to Communism that Orwell expresses is not to be minimized, but he is not undertaking to give us the delusive comfort of moral superiority to an antagonist. He does not separate Russia from the general tendency of the world today. He is saying, indeed, something no less comprehensive than this: that Russia, with its idealistic social revolution now developed into a police state, is but the image of the impending future and that the ultimate threat to human freedom may well come from a similar and even more massive development of the social idealism of our democratic culture. To many liberals, this idea will be incomprehensible, or, if it is understood at all, it will be condemned by them as both foolish and dangerous. We have dutifully learned to think that tyranny manifests itself chiefly, even solely, in the defense of private property and that the profit motive is the source of all evil. And certainly Orwell does not deny that property is powerful or that it may be ruthless in self-defense. But he sees that, as the tendency of recent history goes, property is no longer in anything like the strong position it once was, and that will and intellect are playing a greater and greater part in human history. To many, this can look only like a clear gain. We naturally identify ourselves with will and intellect; they are the very stuff of humanity, and we prefer not to think of their exercise in any except an ideal way. But Orwell tells us that the final oligarchical revolution of the future, which, once established, could never be escaped or countered, will be made not by men who have property to defend but by men of will and intellect, by "the new aristocracy . . . of bureaucrats, scientists, trade-union organizers, publicity experts, sociologists, teachers, journalists, and professional politicians."

> These people [says the authoritative Goldstein, in his account of the revolution], whose origins lay in the salaried middle class and the upper grades of the working class, had been shaped and brought together by the barren world of monopoly industry and centralized government. As compared with their opposite numbers in past ages, they were less avaricious, less tempted by luxury, hungrier for pure power, and, above all, more conscious of what they were doing and more intent on crushing opposition. This last difference was cardinal.

The whole effort of the culture of the last hundred years has been directed toward teaching us to understand the economic motive as the irrational road to death, and to seek salvation in the rational and the planned. Orwell marks a turn in thought; he asks us to consider whether the triumph of certain forces of the mind, in their naked pride and excess, may not produce a state of things far worse than any we have ever known. He is not the first to raise the question, but he is the first to raise it on truly liberal or radical grounds, with no intention of abating the demand for a just society, and with an overwhelming intensity and passion. This priority makes his book a momentous one.

"1984"—The Mysticism of Cruelty

by *Isaac Deutscher*

Few novels written in this generation have obtained a popularity as great as that of George Orwell's *1984*. Few, if any, have made a similar impact on politics. The title of Orwell's book is a political byword. The terms coined by him—"Newspeak," "Oldspeak," "Mutability of the Past," "Big Brother," "Ministry of Truth," "Thought Police," "Crimethink," "Doublethink," "Hate Week," etc.—have entered the political vocabulary; they occur in most newspaper articles and speeches denouncing Russia and communism. Television and the cinema have familiarized many millions of viewers on both sides of the Atlantic with the menacing face of Big Brother and the nightmare of a supposedly Communist Oceania. The novel has served as a sort of an ideological superweapon in the cold war. As in no other book or document, the convulsive fear of communism, which has swept the West since the end of the Second World War, has been reflected and focused in *1984*.

The cold war has created a "social demand" for such an ideological weapon just as it creates the demand for physical superweapons. But the superweapons are genuine feats of technology; and there can be no discrepancy between the uses to which they may be put and the intention of their producers: they are meant to spread death or at least to threaten utter destruction. A book like *1984* may be used without much regard for the author's intention. Some of its features may be torn out of their context, while others, which do not suit the political purpose which the book is made to serve, are ignored or virtually suppressed. Nor need a book like *1984* be a literary masterpiece or even an

---

" '*1984*'—*The Mysticism of Cruelty.*" *From* Russia in Transition, *by Isaac Deutscher (New York: Coward McCann, 1957), pp. 230–45. Copyright 1955 by Isaac Deutscher. [Published in England as* Heretics and Renegades *(London: Hamish Hamilton, 1955)]. Reprinted by permission of Bobbs-Merrill Company, Inc. and Jonathan Cape Ltd.*

important and original work to make its impact. Indeed a work of great literary merit is usually too rich in its texture and too subtle in thought and form to lend itself to adventitious exploitation. As a rule, its symbols cannot easily be transformed into hypnotizing bogies, or its ideas turned into slogans. The words of a great poet when they enter the political vocabulary do so by a process of slow, almost imperceptible infiltration, not by a frantic incursion. The literary masterpiece influences the political mind by fertilizing and enriching it from the inside, not by stunning it.

1984 is the work of an intense and concentrated, but also fear-ridden and restricted imagination. A hostile critic has dismissed it as a "political horror-comic." This is not a fair description: there are in Orwell's novel certain layers of thought and feeling which raise it well above that level. But it is a fact that the symbolism of *1984* is crude; that its chief symbol, Big Brother, resembles the bogieman of a rather inartistic nursery tale; and that Orwell's story unfolds like the plot of a science-fiction film of the cheaper variety, with mechanical horror piling up on mechanical horror so much that, in the end, Orwell's subtler ideas, his pity for his characters, and his satire on the society of his own days (not of 1984) may fail to communicate themselves to the reader. *1984* does not seem to justify the description of Orwell as the modern Swift, a description for which *Animal Farm* provides some justification. Orwell lacks the richness and subtlety of thought and the philosophical detachment of the great satirist. His imagination is ferocious and at times penetrating, but it lacks width, suppleness, and originality.

The lack of originality is illustrated by the fact that Orwell borrowed the idea of *1984*, the plot, the chief characters, the symbols, and the whole climate of his story from a Russian writer who has remained almost unknown in the West. That writer is Evgenii Zamyatin, and the title of the book which served Orwell as the model is *We*. Like *1984*, *We* is an "anti-Utopia," a nightmare vision of the shape of things to come, and a Cassandra cry. Orwell's work is a thoroughly English variation on Zamyatin's theme; and it is perhaps only the thoroughness of Orwell's English approach that gives to his work the originality that it possesses.

A few words about Zamyatin may not be out of place here: there are some points of resemblance in the life stories of the two writers. Zamyatin belonged to an older generation: he was born in 1884 and died in 1937. His early writings, like some of Orwell's, were realistic descriptions of the lower middle class. In his experience the Russian revolution of 1905 played approximately the same role that the Spanish civil war played in Orwell's. He participated in the revolutionary movement, was a member of the Russian Social Democratic Party (to which

Bolsheviks and Mensheviks then still belonged), and was persecuted by the Czarist police. At the ebb of the revolution, he succumbed to a mood of "cosmic pessimism"; and he severed his connection with the Socialist Party, a thing which Orwell, less consistent and to the end influenced by a lingering loyalty to socialism, did not do. In 1917 Zamyatin viewed the new revolution with cold and disillusioned eyes, convinced that nothing good would come out of it. After a brief imprisonment, he was allowed by the Bolshevik government to go abroad; and it was as an émigré in Paris that he wrote *We* in the early 1920's.

The assertion that Orwell borrowed the main elements of *1984* from Zamyatin is not the guess of a critic with a foible for tracing literary influences. Orwell knew Zamyatin's novel and was fascinated by it. He wrote an essay about it, which appeared in the left-socialist *Tribune*, of which Orwell was Literary Editor, on 4 January 1946, just after the publication of *Animal Farm* and before he began writing *1984*. The essay is remarkable not only as a conclusive piece of evidence, supplied by Orwell himself, on the origin of *1984*, but also as a commentary on the idea underlying both *We* and *1984*.

The essay begins with Orwell saying that after having for years looked in vain for Zamyatin's novel, he had at last obtained it in a French edition (under the title *Nous Autres*), and that he was surprised that it had not been published in England, although an American edition had appeared without arousing much interest. "So far as I can judge," Orwell went on, "it is not a book of the first order, but it is certainly an unusual one, and it is astonishing that no English publisher has been enterprising enough to re-issue it." (He concluded the essay with the words: "This is a book to look out for when an English version appears.")

Orwell noticed that Aldous Huxley's *Brave New World* "must be partly derived" from Zamyatin's novel and wondered why this had "never been pointed out." Zamyatin's book was, in his view, much superior and more "relevant to our own situation" than Huxley's. It dealt "with the rebellion of the primitive human spirit against a rationalized, mechanized, painless world."

"Painless" is not the right adjective: the world of Zamyatin's vision is as full of horrors as is that of *1984*. Orwell himself produced in his essay a succinct catalogue of those horrors so that his essay reads now like a synopsis of *1984*. The members of the society described by Zamyatin, says Orwell, "have so completely lost their individuality as to be known only by numbers. They live in glass houses . . . which enables the political police, known as the 'Guardians,' to supervise them more easily. They all wear identical uniforms, and a human being is com-

monly referred to either as 'a number' or a 'unif' (uniform)." Orwell
remarks in parenthesis that Zamyatin wrote "before television was invented." In *1984* this technological refinement is brought in as well as
the helicopters from which the police supervise the homes of the citizens of Oceania in the opening passages of the novel. The "unifs"
suggest the "Proles." In Zamyatin's society of the future as in *1984*
love is forbidden: sexual intercourse is strictly rationed and permitted
only as an unemotional act. "The Single State is ruled over by a person known as the Benefactor," the obvious prototype of Big Brother.
"The guiding principle of the State is that happiness and freedom
are incompatible . . . the Single State has restored his [man's] happiness by removing his freedom." Orwell describes Zamyatin's chief character as "a sort of Utopian Billy Brown of London town" who is "constantly horrified by the atavistic impulses which seize upon him." In
Orwell's novel that Utopian Billy Brown is christened Winston Smith,
and his problem is the same.

For the main *motif* of his plot Orwell is similarly indebted to the
Russian writer. This is how Orwell defines it: "In spite of education
and the vigilance of the Guardians, many of the ancient human instincts are still there." Zamyatin's chief character "falls in love (this is
a crime, of course) with a certain I-330" just as Winston Smith commits
the crime of falling in love with Julia. In Zamyatin's as in Orwell's
story the love affair is mixed up with the hero's participation in an
"underground resistance movement." Zamyatin's rebels "apart from
plotting the overthrow of the State, even indulge, at the moment when
their curtains are down, in such vices as smoking cigarettes and drinking alcohol"; Winston Smith and Julia indulge in drinking "real coffee
with real sugar" in their hideout over Mr. Charrington's shop. In both
novels the crime and the conspiracy are, of course, discovered by the
Guardians or the Thought Police; and in both the hero "is ultimately
saved from the consequences of his own folly."

The combination of "cure" and torture by which Zamyatin's and
Orwell's rebels are "freed" from the atavistic impulses, until they begin
to love Benefactor or Big Brother, is very much the same. In Zamyatin:
"The authorities announce that they have discovered the cause of the
recent disorders: it is that some human beings suffer from a disease
called imagination. The nerve centre responsible for imagination has
now been located, and the disease can be cured by X-ray treatment.
D-503 undergoes the operation, after which it is easy for him to do
what he has known all along that he ought to do—that is, betray his
confederates to the police." In both novels the act of confession and
the betrayal of the woman the hero loves are the curative shocks.

Orwell quotes the following scene of torture from Zamyatin:

"She looked at me, her hands clasping the arms of the chair, until her eyes were completely shut. They took her out, brought her to herself by means of an electric shock, and put her under the bell again. This operation was repeated three times, and not a word issued from her lips."

In Orwell's scenes of torture the "electric shocks" and the "arms of the chair" recur quite often, but Orwell is far more intense, masochistic-sadistic, in his descriptions of cruelty and pain. For instance:

"Without any warning except a slight movement of O'Brien's hand, a wave of pain flooded his body. It was a frightening pain, because he could not see what was happening, and he had the feeling that some mortal injury was being done to him. He did not know whether the thing was really happening, or whether the effect was electrically produced; but his body had been wrenched out of shape, the joints were being slowly torn apart. Although the pain had brought the sweat out on his forehead, the worst of all was the fear that his backbone was about to snap. He set his teeth and breathed hard through his nose, trying to keep silent as long as possible."

The list of Orwell's borrowings is far from complete; but let us now turn from the plot of the two novels to their underlying idea. Taking up the comparison between Zamyatin and Huxley, Orwell says: "It is this intuitive grasp of the irrational side of totalitarianism—human sacrifice, cruelty as an end in itself, the worship of a Leader who is credited with divine attributes—that makes Zamyatin's book superior to Huxley's." It is this, we may add, that made of it Orwell's model. Criticizing Huxley, Orwell writes that he could find no clear reason why the society of *Brave New World* should be so rigidly and elaborately stratified: "The aim is not economic exploitation. . . . *There is no power-hunger, no sadism, no hardness of any kind.* Those at the top have no strong motive for staying on the top, and though everyone is happy in a vacuous way, life has become so pointless that it is difficult to believe that such a society could endure." (My italics.) In contrast, the society of Zamyatin's anti-Utopia could endure, in Orwell's view, because in it the supreme motive of action and the reason for social stratification are not economic exploitation, for which there is no need, but precisely the "power-hunger, sadism, and hardness" of those who "stay at the top." It is easy to recognize in this the *leitmotif* of *1984*.

In Oceania technological development has reached so high a level that society could well satisfy all its material needs and establish equality in its midst. But inequality and poverty are maintained in order to keep Big Brother in power. In the past, says Orwell, dictatorship safeguarded inequality, now inequality safeguards dictatorship. But what purpose does the dictatorship itself serve? "The party seeks power entirely for its own sake. . . . Power is not a means, it is an end. One does not establish a dictatorship in order to safeguard a revolution; one makes the revolution in order to establish the dictatorship. The object of persecution is persecution. . . . The object of power is power."

Orwell wondered whether Zamyatin did "intend the Soviet regime to be the special target of his satire." He was not sure of this: "What Zamyatin seems to be aiming at is not any particular country but the implied aims of the industrial civilization. . . . It is evident from *We* that he had a strong leaning towards primitivism. . . . *We* is in effect a study of the Machine, the genie that man has thoughtlessly let out of its bottle and cannot put back again." The same ambiguity of the author's aim is evident also in *1984*.

Orwell's guess about Zamyatin was correct. Though Zamyatin was opposed to the Soviet regime, it was not exclusively, or even mainly, that regime which he satirized. As Orwell rightly remarked, the early Soviet Russia had few features in common with the supermechanized State of Zamyatin's anti-Utopia. That writer's leaning towards primitivism was in line with a Russian tradition, with Slavophilism and hostility towards the bourgeois West, with the glorification of the *muzhik* and of the old patriarchal Russia, with Tolstoy and Dostoyevsky. Even as an émigré, Zamyatin was disillusioned with the West in the characteristically Russian fashion. At times he seemed half-reconciled with the Soviet regime when it was already producing its Benefactor in the person of Stalin. In so far as he directed the darts of his satire against Bolshevism, he did so on the ground that Bolshevism was bent on replacing the old primitive Russia by the modern, mechanized society. Curiously enough, he set his story in the year 2600; and he seemed to say to the Bolsheviks: this is what Russia will look like if you succeed in giving to your regime the background of Western technology. In Zamyatin, as in some other Russian intellectuals disillusioned with socialism, the hankering after the primitive modes of thought and life was in so far natural as primitivism was still strongly alive in the Russian background.

In Orwell there was and there could be no such authentic nostalgia after the preindustrial society. Primitivism had no part in his experience and background, except during his stay in Burma, when he was hardly attracted by it. But he was terrified of the uses to which technology might be put by men determined to enslave society; and so he, too, came to question and satirize "the implied aims of industrial civilization."

Although his satire is more recognizably aimed at Soviet Russia than

Zamyatin's, Orwell saw elements of Oceania in the England of his own days as well, not to speak of the United States. Indeed, the society of *1984* embodies all that he hated and disliked in his own surroundings: the drabness and monotony of the English industrial suburb, the "filthy and grimy and smelly" ugliness of which he tried to match in his naturalistic, repetitive, and oppressive style; the food rationing and the government controls which he knew in wartime Britain; the "rubbishy newspapers containing almost nothing except sport, crime, and astrology, sensational five-cent novelettes, films oozing with sex"; and so on. Orwell knew well that newspapers of this sort did not exist in Stalinist Russia, and that the faults of the Stalinist press were of an altogether different kind. *Newspeak* is much less a satire on the Stalinist idiom than on Anglo-American journalistic "cablese," which he loathed and with which, as a working journalist, he was well familiar.

It is easy to tell which features of the party of *1984* satirize the British Labour Party rather than the Soviet Communist Party. Big Brother and his followers make no attempt to indoctrinate the working class, an omission Orwell would have been the last to ascribe to Stalinism. His Proles "vegetate": "heavy work, petty quarrels, films, gambling . . . fill their mental horizon." Like the rubbishy newspapers and the films oozing with sex, so gambling, the new opium of the people, does not belong to the Russian scene. The Ministry of Truth is a transparent caricature of London's wartime Ministry of Information. The monster of Orwell's vision is, like every nightmare, made up of all sorts of faces and features and shapes, familiar and unfamiliar. Orwell's talent and originality are evident in the domestic aspect of his satire. But in the vogue which *1984* has enjoyed that aspect has rarely been noticed.

1984 is a document of dark disillusionment not only with Stalinism but with every form and shade of socialism. It is a cry from the abyss of despair. What plunged Orwell into that abyss? It was without any doubt the spectacle of the Stalinist Great Purges of 1936–1938, the repercussions of which he experienced in Catalonia. As a man of sensitivity and integrity, he could not react to the purges otherwise than with anger and horror. His conscience could not be soothed by the Stalinist justifications and sophisms which at the time did soothe the conscience of, for instance, Arthur Koestler, a writer of greater brilliance and sophistication but of less moral resolution. The Stalinist justifications and sophisms were both *beneath* and *above* Orwell's level of reasoning—they were beneath and above the common sense and the stubborn empiricism of Billy Brown of London town, with whom Orwell identified himself even in his most rebellious or revolutionary moments. He was outraged, shocked, and shaken in his beliefs. He had

never been a member of the Communist Party. But, as an adherent of
the semi-Trotskyist P.O.U.M., he had, despite all his reservations,
tacitly assumed a certain community of purpose and solidarity with the
Soviet regime through all its vicissitudes and transformations, which
were to him somewhat obscure and exotic.

The purges and their Spanish repercussions not only destroyed that
community of purpose. Not only did he see the gulf between Stalinists
and anti-Stalinists opening suddenly inside embattled Republican
Spain. This, the immediate effect of the purges, was overshadowed by
"the irrational side of totalitarianism—human sacrifice, cruelty as an
end in itself, the worship of a Leader," and "the color of the sinister
slave-civilizations of the ancient world" spreading over contemporary
society.

Like most British socialists, Orwell had never been a Marxist. The
dialectical-materialist philosophy had always been too abstruse for him.
From instinct rather than consciousness he had been a stanch rationalist. The distinction between the Marxist and the rationalist is of some
importance. Contrary to an opinion widespread in Anglo-Saxon countries, Marxism is not at all rationalist in its philosophy: it does not
assume that human beings are, as a rule, guided by rational motives
and that they can be argued into socialism by reason. Marx himself
begins *Das Kapital* with the elaborate philosophical and historical inquiry into the "fetishistic" modes of thought and behavior rooted in
"commodity production"—that is, in man's work for, and dependence
on, a market. The class struggle, as Marx describes it, is anything but
a rational process. This does not prevent the rationalists of socialism
from describing themselves sometimes as Marxists. But the authentic
Marxist may claim to be mentally better prepared than the rationalist
is for the manifestations of irrationality in human affairs, even for such
manifestations as Stalin's Great Purges. He may feel upset or mortified
by them, but he need not feel shaken in his *Weltanschauung,* while the
rationalist is lost and helpless when the irrationality of the human
existence suddenly stares him in the face. If he clings to his rationalism,
reality eludes him. If he pursues reality and tries to grasp it, he must
part with his rationalism.

Orwell pursued reality and found himself bereft of his conscious and
unconscious assumptions about life. In his thoughts he could not
henceforth get away from the Purges. Directly and indirectly, they supplied the subject matter for nearly all that he wrote after his Spanish
experience. This was an honorable obsession, the obsession of a mind
not inclined to cheat itself comfortably and to stop grappling with an
alarming moral problem. But grappling with the Purges, his mind
became infected by their irrationality. He found himself incapable of

explaining what was happening in terms which were familiar to him, the terms of empirical common sense. Abandoning rationalism, he increasingly viewed reality through the dark glasses of a quasi-mystical pessimism.

It has been said that *1984* is the figment of the imagination of a dying man. There is some truth in this, but not the whole truth. It was indeed with the last feverish flicker of life in him that Orwell wrote this book. Hence the extraordinary, gloomy intensity of his vision and language, and the almost physical immediacy with which he suffered the tortures which his creative imagination was inflicting on his chief character. He identified his own withering physical existence with the decayed and shrunken body of Winston Smith, to whom he imparted and in whom he invested, as it were, his own dying pangs. He projected the last spasms of his own suffering into the last pages of his last book. But the main explanation of the inner logic of Orwell's disillusionment and pessimism lies not in the writer's death agonies, but in the experience and the thought of the living man and in his convulsive reaction from his defeated rationalism.

"I understand HOW: I do not understand WHY" is the refrain of *1984*. Winston Smith knows how Oceania functions and how its elaborate mechanism of tyranny works, but he does not know what is its ultimate cause and ultimate purpose. He turns for the answer to the pages of "*the* book," the mysterious classic of *Crimethink*, the authorship of which is attributed to Emmanuel Goldstein, the inspirer of the conspiratorial Brotherhood. But he manages to read through only those chapters of "*the* book" which deal with the HOW. The Thought Police descend upon him just when he is about to begin reading the chapters which promise to explain WHY; and so the question remains unanswered.

This was Orwell's own predicament. He asked the Why not so much about the Oceania of his vision as about Stalinism and the Great Purges. At one point he certainly turned for the answer to Trotsky: it was from Trotsky-Bronstein that he took the few sketchy biographical data and even the physiognomy and the Jewish name for Emmanuel Goldstein; and the fragments of "*the* book," which take up so many pages in *1984*, are an obvious, though not very successful, paraphrase of Trotsky's *The Revolution Betrayed*. Orwell was impressed by Trotsky's moral grandeur and at the same time he partly distrusted it and partly doubted its authenticity. The ambivalence of his view of Trotsky finds its counterpart in Winston Smith's attitude towards Goldstein. To the end Smith cannot find out whether Goldstein and the Brotherhood have ever existed in reality, and whether "*the* book" was not concocted by the Thought Police. The barrier between Trotsky's thought and

himself, a barrier which Orwell could never break down, was Marxism
and dialectical materialism. He found in Trotsky the answer to How,
not to Why.

But Orwell could not content himself with historical agnosticism.
He was anything but a skeptic. His mental makeup was rather that of
the fanatic, determined to get an answer, a quick and a plain answer, to
his question. He was now tense with distrust and suspicion and on the
lookout for the dark conspiracies hatched by *them* against the decen-
cies of Billy Brown of London town. *They* were the Nazis, the Stalinists, and—Churchill and Roosevelt, and ultimately all who had any
raison d'état to defend, for at heart Orwell was a simple-minded anarchist and, in his eyes, any political movement forfeited its *raison
d'être* the moment it acquired a *raison d'état*. To analyze a complicated
social background, to try and unravel tangles of political motives, cal-
culations, fears and suspicions, and to discern the compulsion of circumstances behind *their* action was beyond him. Generalizations about
social forces, social trends, and historic inevitabilities made him bristle
with suspicion. Yet, without some such generalizations, properly and
sparingly used, no realistic answer could be given to the question
which preoccupied Orwell. His gaze was fixed on the trees, or rather on
a single tree, in front of him, and he was almost blind to the wood.
Yet his distrust of historical generalizations led him in the end to adopt
and to cling to the oldest, the most banal, the most abstract, the most
metaphysical, and the most barren of all generalizations: all *their* conspiracies and plots and purges and diplomatic deals had one source and
one source only—"sadistic power-hunger." Thus he made his jump
from workaday, rationalistic common sense to the mysticism of cruelty
which inspires *1984*.[1]

[1] This opinion is based on personal reminiscences as well as on an analysis of Orwell's work. During the last war Orwell seemed attracted by the critical, then somewhat unusual, tenor of my commentaries on Russia which appeared in *The Econo-
mist*, *The Observer*, and *Tribune*. (Later we were both *The Observer*'s correspond-
ents in Germany and occasionally shared a room in a press camp.) However, it took
me little time to become aware of the differences of approach behind our seeming
agreement. I remember that I was taken aback by the stubbornness with which
Orwell dwelt on "conspiracies," and that his political reasoning struck me as a
Freudian sublimation of persecution mania. He was, for instance, unshakably convinced that Stalin, Churchill, and Roosevelt consciously plotted to divide the world,
and to divide it for good, among themselves, and to subjugate it in common. (I can
trace the idea of Oceania, Eastasia, and Eurasia back to that time.) "*They* are all
power-hungry," he used to repeat. When once I pointed out to him that underneath
the apparent solidarity of the Big Three one could discern clearly the conflict between them, already coming to the surface, Orwell was so startled and incredulous
that he at once related our conversation in his column in *Tribune*, and added that
he saw no sign of the approach of the conflict of which I spoke. This was at the

In *1984* man's mastery over the machine has reached so high a level that society is in a position to produce plenty for everybody and put an end to inequality. But poverty and inequality are maintained only to satisfy the sadistic urges of Big Brother. Yet we do not even know whether Big Brother really exists—he may be only a myth. It is the collective cruelty of the party (not necessarily of its individual members who may be intelligent and well-meaning people), that torments Oceania. Totalitarian society is ruled by a disembodied sadism. Orwell imagined that he had "transcended" the familiar and, as he thought, increasingly irrelevant concepts of social class and class interest. But in these Marxist generalizations, the interest of a social class bears at least some specific relation to the individual interests and the social position of its members, even if the class interest does not represent a simple sum of the individual interests. In Orwell's party the whole bears no relation to the parts. The party is not a social body actuated by any interest or purpose. It is a phantomlike emanation of all that is foul in human nature. It is the metaphysical, mad and triumphant, Ghost of Evil.

Of course, Orwell intended *1984* as a warning. But the warning defeats itself because of its underlying boundless despair. Orwell saw totalitarianism as bringing history to a standstill. Big Brother is invincible: "If you want a picture of the future, imagine a boot stamping on a human face—for ever." He projected the spectacle of the Great Purges on to the future, and he saw it fixed there forever, because he was not capable of grasping the events realistically, in their complex historical context. To be sure, the events were highly "irrational"; but he who because of this treats them irrationally is very much like the psychiatrist whose mind becomes unhinged by dwelling too closely with insanity. *1984* is in effect not so much a warning as a piercing shriek announcing the advent of the Black Millennium, the millennium of damnation.

The shriek, amplified by all the "mass-media" of our time, has frightened millions of people. But it has not helped them to see more clearly the issues with which the world is grappling; it has not advanced their understanding. It has only increased and intensified the waves of panic and hate that run through the world and obfuscate innocent minds. *1984* has taught millions to look at the conflict between East and West

---

time of the Yalta conference, or shortly thereafter, when not much foresight was needed to see what was coming. What struck me in Orwell was his lack of historical sense and of psychological insight into political life coupled with an acute, though narrow, penetration into some aspects of politics and with an incorruptible firmness of conviction.

in terms of black and white, and it has shown them a monster bogy and a monster scapegoat for all the ills that plague mankind.

At the onset of the atomic age, the world is living in a mood of Apocalyptic horror. That is why millions of people respond so passionately to the Apocalyptic vision of a novelist. The Apocalyptic atomic and hydrogen monsters, however, have not been let loose by Big Brother. The chief predicament of contemporary society is that it has not yet succeeded in adjusting its way of life and its social and political institutions to the prodigious advance of its technological knowledge. We do not know what has been the impact of the atomic and hydrogen bombs on the thoughts of millions in the East, where anguish and fear may be hidden behind the façade of a facile (or perhaps embarrassed?) official optimism. But it would be dangerous to blind ourselves to the fact that in the West millions of people may be inclined, in their anguish and fear, to flee from their own responsibility for mankind's destiny and to vent their anger and despair on the giant Bogy-cum-Scapegoat which Orwell's *1984* has done so much to place before their eyes.

"Have you read this book? You must read it, sir. Then you will know why we must drop the atom bomb on the Bolshies!" With these words a blind, miserable newsvender recommended to me *1984* in New York, a few weeks before Orwell's death.

Poor Orwell, could he ever imagine that his own book would become so prominent an item in the program of Hate Week?

1984: History as Nightmare

by Irving Howe

About some books we feel that our reluctance to return to them is the true measure of our admiration. It is hard to suppose that many people go back, from a spontaneous desire, to reread *1984*: there is neither reason nor need to, no one forgets it. The usual distinctions between forgotten details and a vivid general impression mean nothing here, for the book is written out of one passionate breath, each word is bent to a severe discipline of meaning, everything is stripped to the bareness of terror.

Kafka's *The Trial* is also a book of terror, but it is a paradigm and to some extent a puzzle, so that one may lose oneself in the rhythm of the paradigm and play with the parts of the puzzle. Kafka's novel persuades us that life is inescapably hazardous and problematic, but the very "universality" of this idea helps soften its impact: to apprehend the terrible on the plane of metaphysics is to lend it an almost soothing aura. And besides, *The Trial* absorbs one endlessly in its aspect of enigma.

Though not nearly so great a book, *1984* is in some ways more terrible. For it is not a paradigm and hardly a puzzle; whatever enigmas it raises concern not the imagination of the author but the life of our time. It does not take us away from, or beyond, our obsession with immediate social reality, and in reading the book we tend to say—the linguistic clumsiness conceals a deep truth—that the world of 1984 is "more real" than our own. The book appals us because its terror, far from being inherent in the "human condition," is particular to our century; what haunts us is the sickening awareness that in *1984* Orwell has seized upon those elements of our public life that, given courage and intelligence, were avoidable.

How remarkable a book *1984* really is, can be discovered only after a second reading. It offers true testimony, it speaks for our time. And because it derives from a perception of how our time may end, the book trembles with an eschatological fury that is certain to create among its readers, even those who sincerely believe they admire it, the most powerful kinds of resistance. It already has. Openly in England, more cautiously in America, there has arisen a desire among intellectuals to belittle Orwell's achievement, often in the guise of celebrating his humanity and his "goodness." They feel embarrassed before the apocalyptic desperation of the book, they begin to wonder whether it may not be just a little overdrawn and humorless, they even suspect it is tinged with the hysteria of the death-bed. Nor can it be denied that all of us would feel more comfortable if the book could be cast out. It is a remarkable book.

Whether it is a remarkable novel or a novel at all, seems unimportant. It is not, I suppose, really a novel, or at least it does not satisfy those expectations we have come to have with regard to the novel—expectations that are mainly the heritage of nineteenth century romanticism with its stress upon individual consciousness, psychological analysis and the study of intimate relations. One American critic, a serious critic, reviewed the book under the heading, "Truth Maybe, Not Fiction," as if thereby to demonstrate the strictness with which he held to distinctions of literary genre. Actually, he was demonstrating a certain narrowness of modern taste, for such a response of *1984* is possible only when discriminations are no longer made between fiction and the novel, which is but one kind of fiction though the kind modern readers care for most.

A cultivated eighteenth century reader would never have said of *1984* that it may be true but isn't fiction, for it was then understood that fiction, like poetry, can have many modes and be open to many mixtures; the novel had not yet established its popular tyranny. What is more, the style of *1984,* which many readers take to be drab or uninspired or "sweaty," would have been appreciated by someone like Defoe, since Defoe would have immediately understood how the pressures of Orwell's subject, like the pressures of his own, demand a gritty and hammering factuality. The style of *1984* is the style of a man whose commitment to a dreadful vision is at war with the nausea to which that vision reduces him. So acute is this conflict that delicacies of phrasing or displays of rhetoric come to seem frivolous—*he has no time, he must get it all down.* Those who fail to see this, I am convinced, have succumbed to the pleasant tyrannies of estheticism; they have allowed their fondness for a cultivated style to blind them to the urgencies of prophetic expression. The last thing Orwell cared about when he wrote *1984*, the last thing he should have cared about, was literature.

Another complaint one often hears is that there are no credible or "three-dimensional" characters in the book. Apart from its rather facile identification of credibility with a particular treatment of character, the complaint involves a failure to see that in some books an extended amount of psychological specification or even dramatic incident can be disastrous. In *1984* Orwell is trying to present the kind of world in which individuality has become obsolete and personality a crime. The whole idea of the self as something precious and inviolable is a *cultural* idea, and as we understand it, a product of the liberal era; but Orwell has imagined a world in which the self, whatever subterranean existence it manages to eke out, is no longer a significant value, not even a value to be violated.

Winston Smith and Julia come through as rudimentary figures because they are slowly learning, and at great peril to themselves, what it means to be human. Their experiment in the rediscovery of the human, which is primarily an experiment in the possibilities of solitude, leads them to cherish two things that are fundamentally hostile to the totalitarian outlook: a life of contemplativeness and the joy of "purposeless"—that is, free—sexual passion. But this experiment cannot go very far, as they themselves know; it is inevitable that they be caught and destroyed.

Partly, that is the meaning and the pathos of the book. Were it possible, in the world of 1984, to show human character in anything resembling genuine freedom, in its play of spontaneous desire and caprice—it would not be the world of 1984. So that in a slightly obtuse way the complaint that Orwell's characters seem thin testifies to the strength of the book, for it is a complaint directed not against his technique but against his primary assumptions.

The book cannot be understood, nor can it be properly valued, simply by resorting to the usual literary categories, for it posits a situation in which these categories are no longer significant. Everything has hardened into politics, the leviathan has swallowed man. About such a world it is, strictly speaking, impossible to write a novel, if only because the human relationships taken for granted in the novel are here suppressed.[1] The book must first be approached through politics, yet

[1] Some people have suggested that *1984* is primarily a symptom of Orwell's psychological condition, the nightmare of a disturbed man who suffered from paranoid fantasies, was greatly troubled by dirt, and feared that sexual contact would bring down punishment from those in authority. Apart from its intolerable glibness, such an "explanation" explains either too much or too little. Almost everyone has night-

not as a political study or treatise. It is something else, at once a model and a vision—a model of the totalitarian state in its "pure" or "essential" form and a vision of what this state can do to human life. Yet the theme of the conflict between ideology and emotion, as at times their fusion and mutual reinforcement, is still to be found in *1984*, as a dim underground motif. Without this theme, there could be no dramatic conflict in a work of fiction dominated by politics. Winston Smith's effort to reconstruct the old tune about the bells of St. Clement is a token of his desire to regain the condition of humanness, which is here nothing more than a capacity for so "useless" a feeling as nostalgia. Between the tune and Oceania there can be no peace.

1984 projects a nightmare in which politics has displaced humanity and the state has stifled society. In a sense, it is a profoundly antipolitical book, full of hatred for the kind of world in which public claims destroy the possibilities for private life; and this conservative side of Orwell's outlook he suggests, perhaps unconsciously, through the first name of his hero. But if the image of Churchill is thus raised in order to celebrate, a little wryly, the memory of the bad (or as Winston Smith comes to feel, the good) old days, the opposing image of Trotsky is raised, a little skeptically, in order to discover the inner meanings of totalitarian society. When Winston Smith learns to think of Oceania as a *problem*—which is itself to commit a "crimethink"—he turns to the forbidden work of Emmanuel Goldstein, *The Theory and Practise of Oligarchical Collectivism,* clearly a replica of Trotsky's *The Revolution Betrayed.* The power and intelligence of *1984* partly derives from a tension between these images; even as Orwell understood the need for politics in the modern world, he felt a profound distaste for the ways of political life, and he was honest enough not to try to suppress one or another side of this struggle within himself.

II

No other book has succeeded so completely in rendering the essential quality of totalitarianism. *1984* is limited in scope; it does not pretend to investigate the genesis of the totalitarian state, nor the laws of its economy, nor the prospect for its survival; it simply evokes the "tone" of life in a totalitarian society. And since it is not a realistic novel, it

---

mares and a great many people have ambiguous feelings about sex, but few manage to write books with the power of *1984*. Nightmare the book may be, and no doubt it is grounded, as are all books, in the psychological troubles of its author. But it is also grounded in his psychological health, otherwise it could not penetrate so deeply the social reality of our time. The private nightmare, if it is there, is profoundly related to, and helps us understand, public events.

can treat Oceania as an *extreme instance,* one that might never actually exist but which illuminates the nature of societies that do exist.[2]

Orwell's profoundest insight is that in a totalitarian world man's life is shorn of dynamic possibilities. The end of life is completely predictable in its beginning, the beginning merely a manipulated preparation for the end. There is no opening for surprise, for that spontaneous animation which is the token of and justification for freedom. Oceanic society may evolve through certain stages of economic development, but the life of its members is static, a given and measured quantity that can neither rise to tragedy nor tumble to comedy. Human personality, as we have come to grasp for it in a class society and hope for it in a classless society, is obliterated; man becomes a function of a process he is never allowed to understand or control. The fetishism of the state replaces the fetishism of commodities.

There have, of course, been unfree societies in the past, yet in most of them it was possible to find an oasis of freedom, if only because none had the resources to enforce total consent. But totalitarianism, which represents a decisive break from the Western tradition, aims to permit no such luxuries; it offers a total "solution" to the problems of the twentieth century, that is, a total distortion of what might be a solution. To be sure, no totalitarian state has been able to reach this degree of "perfection," which Orwell, like a physicist who in his experiment assumes the absence of friction, has assumed for Oceania. But the knowledge that friction can never actually be absent does not make the experiment any the less valuable.

To the degree that the totalitarian state approaches its "ideal" condition, it destroys the margin for unforeseen behavior; as a character in Dostoevsky's *The Possessed* remarks, "only the necessary is necessary." Nor is there a social crevice in which the recalcitrant or independent mind can seek shelter. The totalitarian state assumes that—given modern technology, complete political control, the means of terror and a rationalized contempt for moral tradition—anything is possible. Anything can be done with men, anything with their minds, with history and with words. Reality is no longer something to be acknowledged or experienced or even transformed; it is fabricated according to the need and will of the state, sometimes in anticipation of the future, sometimes as a retrospective improvement upon the past.

But even as Orwell, overcoming the resistance of his own nausea,

---

[2] "My novel *1984,*" wrote Orwell shortly before his death, "is *not* intended as an attack on socialism, or on the British Labor Party, but as a show-up of the perversions to which a centralized economy is liable. . . . I do not believe that the kind of society I describe necessarily *will* arrive, but I believe . . . that something resembling it *could* arrive."

evoked the ethos of the totalitarian world, he used very little of what is ordinarily called "imagination" in order to show how this ethos stains every aspect of human life. Like most good writers, he understood that imagination is primarily the capacity for apprehending reality, for seeing both clearly and deeply whatever it is that exists. That is why his vision of social horror, if taken as a model rather than a portrait, strikes one as essentially credible, while the efforts of most writers to create utopias or anti-utopias founder precisely on their desire to be scientific or inventive. Orwell understood that social horror consists not in the prevalence of diabolical machines or in the invasion of Martian automatons flashing death rays from mechanical eyes, but in the persistence of inhuman relations among men.

And he understood, as well, the significance of what I can only call the psychology and politics of "one more step." From a bearable neurosis to a crippling psychosis, from a decayed society in which survival is still possible to a totalitarian state in which it is hardly desirable, there may be only "one step." To lay bare the logic of that social regression which leads to totalitarianism Orwell had merely to allow his imagination to take . . . one step.

Consider such typical aspects of Oceanic society as telescreens and the use of children as informers against their parents. There are no telescreens in Russia, but there could well be: nothing in Russian society contradicts the "principle" of telescreens. Informing against parents who are political heretics is not a common practice in the United States, but some people have been deprived of their jobs on the charge of having maintained "prolonged associations" with their parents. To capture the totalitarian spirit, Orwell had merely to allow certain tendencies in modern society to spin forward without the brake of sentiment or humaneness. He could thus make clear the relationship between his model of totalitarianism and the societies we know in our experience, and he could do this without resorting to the clap-trap of science fiction or the crude assumption that we already live in 1984. In imagining the world of 1984 he took only one step, and because he knew how long and terrible a step it was, he had no need to take another.

III

Through a struggle of the mind and an effort of the will that clearly left him exhausted, Orwell came to see—which is far more than simply to understand—what the inner spirit or ethos of totalitarianism is. But it was characteristic of Orwell as a writer that he felt uneasy with a general idea or a total vision; things took on reality for him only as they were particular and concrete. The world of 1984 seems to have had for him the hallucinatory immediacy that Yoknapatawpha County has for Faulkner or London had for Dickens, and even as he ruthlessly subordinated his descriptions to the dominating theme of the book, Orwell succeeded in noting the details of Oceanic society with a painstaking and sometimes uncanny accuracy.

There are first the incidental accuracies of mimicry. Take, as an example, Orwell's grasp of the role played by the scapegoat-enemy of the totalitarian world, the rituals of hate for which he is indispensable, and more appalling, the uncertainty as to whether he even exists or is a useful fabrication of the state. Among the best passages in the book are those in which Orwell imitates Trotsky's style in *The Theory and Practise of Oligarchical Collectivism*. Orwell caught the rhetorical sweep and grandeur of Trotsky's writing, particularly his fondness for using scientific references in non-scientific contexts: "Even after enormous upheavals and seemingly irrevocable changes, the same pattern has always reasserted itself, just as a gyroscope will always return to equilibrium, however far it is pushed one way or another." And in another sentence Orwell beautifully captured Trotsky's way of using a compressed paradox to sum up the absurdity of a whole society: "The fields are cultivated with horse plows while books are written by machinery."

Equally skillful was Orwell's evocation of the physical atmosphere of Oceania, the overwhelming gloomy shabbiness of its streets and houses, the tasteless sameness of the clothes its people wear, the unappetizing gray-pink stew they eat, that eternal bureaucratic stew which seems to go with all modern oppressive institutions. Orwell had not been taken in by the legend that totalitarianism is at least efficient; instead of the usual chromium-and-skyscraper vision of the future, he painted London in 1984 as a composite of the city in its dismal grayness during the last (Second) world war and of the modern Russian cities with their Victorian ostentation and rotting slums. In all of his books Orwell had shown himself only mildly gifted at visual description but remarkably keen at detecting loathsome and sickening odors. He had the best nose of his generation—his mind sometimes betrayed him, his nose never. In the world of 1984, he seems to be suggesting, all of the rubbish of the past, together with some that no one had quite been able to foresee, is brought together.

The rubbish survived, but what of the past itself, the past in which men had managed to live and sometimes with a little pleasure? One of the most poignant scenes in the book is that in which Winston Smith, trying to discover what life was like before the reign of Big Brother, talks to an old prole in a pub. The exchange is unsatisfactory to Smith,

since the worker can remember only fragments of disconnected fact
and is quite unable to generalize from his memories; but the scene
itself is a fine bit of dramatic action, indicating that not only does
totalitarian society destroy the past through the obliteration of objective records but that it destroys the memory of the past through a disintegration of individual consciousness. The worker with whom Smith
talks remembers that the beer was better before Big Brother (a very
important fact) but he cannot really understand Smith's question: "Do
you feel that you have more freedom now than you had in those days?"
To pose, let alone understand, such a question requires a degree of
social continuity, as well as a set of complex assumptions, which
Oceania is gradually destroying.

The destruction of social memory becomes a major industry in
Oceania, and here of course Orwell was borrowing directly from Stalinism which, as the most "advanced" form of totalitarianism, was infi-
nitely more adept at this job than was fascism. (Hitler burned books,
Stalin had them rewritten.) In Oceania the embarrassing piece of paper
slides down memory hole—and that is all.

Orwell is similarly acute in noticing the relationship between the
totalitarian state and what passes for culture. Novels are produced by
machine; the state anticipates all wants, from "cleansed" versions of
Byron to pornographic magazines; that vast modern industry which
we call "popular culture" has become an important state function.
Meanwhile, the language is stripped of words that suggest refinements
of attitude or gradations of sensibility.

And with feeling as with language. Oceania seeks to blot out spontaneous affection because it assumes, with good reason, that whatever
is uncalculated is subversive. Smith thinks to himself:

> It would not have occurred to [his mother] that an action which is in-
> effectual thereby becomes meaningless. If you loved someone, you loved
> him, and when you had nothing else to give, you still gave him love.
> When the last of the chocolate was gone, his mother had clasped the
> children in her arms. It was no use, it changed nothing, it did not
> produce more chocolate, it did not avert the child's death or her own;
> but it seemed natural for her to do it.

IV

At only a few points can one question Orwell's vision of totalitarianism, and even these involve highly problematic matters. If they are
errors at all, it is only to the extent that they drive valid observations
too hard: Orwell's totalitarian society is at times more *total* than we
can presently imagine.

One such problem has to do with the relation between the state and "human nature." Granted that human nature is itself a cultural concept with a history of change behind it; granted that the pressures of fear and force can produce extreme variations in human conduct. There yet remains the question: to what extent can a terrorist regime suppress or radically alter the fundamental impulses of man? Is there a constant in human nature which no amount of terror or propaganda can destroy?

In Oceania the sexual impulse, while not destroyed, has been remarkably weakened among the members of the Outer Party. For the faithful, sexual energy is transformed into political hysteria. There is a harrowing passage in which Smith remembers his sexual relations with his former wife, a loyal party member who would submit herself once a week, as if for an ordeal and resisting even while insisting, in order to procreate for the party. The only thing she did not feel was pleasure.

Orwell puts the matter with some care:

> The aim of the Party was not merely to prevent men and women from forming loyalties which it might not be able to control. Its real, undeclared purpose was to remove all pleasure from the sexual act. Not love so much as eroticism was the enemy, inside marriage as well as outside it . . . The only recognized purpose of marriage was to beget children for the service of the Party. Sexual intercourse was to be looked on as a slightly disgusting minor operation, like having an enema . . . The Party was trying to kill the sex instinct, or, if it could not be killed, then to distort it and dirty it . . . And so far as the women were concerned, the Party's efforts were largely successful.

That Orwell has here come upon an important tendency in modern life, that the totalitarian state is inherently an enemy of erotic freedom, seems to me indisputable. And we know from the past that the sexual impulse can be heavily suppressed. In Puritan communities, for example, sex was regarded with great suspicion, and it is not hard to imagine that even in marriage the act of love might bring the Puritans very little pleasure. But it should be remembered that in Puritan communities hostility toward sex was interwoven with a powerful faith: men mortified themselves in behalf of God. By contrast, Oceania looks upon faith not merely as suspect but downright dangerous, for its rulers prefer mechanical assent to intellectual fervor or zealous belief. (They have probably read enough history to know that in the Protestant era enthusiasm had a way of turning into individualism.)

Given these circumstances, is it plausible that the Outer Party members would be able to discard erotic pleasure so completely? Is this not cutting too close to the limit of indestructible human needs? I should

think that in a society so pervaded by boredom and grayness as
Oceania is, there would be a pressing hunger for erotic adventure, to
say nothing of experiments in perversion.

A totalitarian society can force people to do many things that violate
their social and physical desires; it may even teach them to receive pain
with quiet resignation; but I doubt that it can break down the fundamental, if sometimes ambiguous, distinction between pleasure and
pain. Man's biological make-up requires him to obtain food, and, with
less regularity or insistence, sex; and while society can do a great deal—
it has—to dim the pleasures of sex and reduce the desire for food, it
seems reasonable to assume that even when consciousness has been
blitzed, the "animal drives" of man cannot be violated as thoroughly
as Orwell suggests. In the long run, these drives may prove to be one
of the most enduring forces of resistance to the totalitarian state.

Does not Orwell imply something of the sort when he shows Winston Smith turning to individual reflection and Julia to private pleasure? What is the source of their rebellion if not the "innate" resistance
of their minds and bodies to the destructive pressures of Oceania? It is
clear that they are no more intelligent or sensitive—certainly no more
heroic—than most Outer Party members. And if their needs as human
beings force these two quite ordinary people to rebellion, may not the
same thing happen to others?

A related problem concerns Orwell's treatment of the workers in
Oceania. The proles, just because they are at the bottom of the heap
and perform routine tasks of work, get off rather better than members
of the Outer Party: they are granted more privacy, the telescreen does
not bawl instructions at them nor watch their every motion, and the
secret police seldom troubles them, except to wipe out a talented or
independent worker. Presumably Orwell would justify this by saying
that the State need no longer fear the workers, so demoralized have
they become as individuals and so powerless as a class. That such a
situation might arise in the future it would be foolhardy to deny, and
in any case Orwell is deliberately pushing things to a dramatic extreme; but we should also notice that nothing of the kind has yet happened, neither the Nazis nor the Stalinists having ever relaxed their
control or surveillance of the workers to any significant extent. Orwell
has here made the mistake of taking more than "one step" and thereby
breaking the tie between the world we know and the world he has
imagined.

But his treatment of the proles can be questioned on more fundamental grounds. The totalitarian state can afford no luxury, allow no
exception; it cannot tolerate the existence of any group beyond the
perimeter of its control; it can never become so secure as to lapse into

indifference. Scouring every corner of society for rebels it knows do not exist, the totalitarian state cannot come to rest for any prolonged period of time. To do so would be to risk disintegration. It must always tend toward a condition of self-agitation, shaking and reshaking its members, testing and retesting them in order to insure its power. And since, as Winston Smith concludes, the proles remain one of the few possible sources of revolt, it can hardly seem plausible that Oceania would permit them even the relative freedom Orwell describes.

Finally, there is Orwell's extremely interesting though questionable view of the dynamics of power in a totalitarian state. As he portrays the party oligarchy in Oceania, it is the first ruling class of modern times to dispense with ideology. It makes no claim to be ruling in behalf of humanity, the workers, the nation or anyone but itself; it rejects as naive the rationale of the Grand Inquisitor that he oppresses the ignorant to accomplish their salvation. O'Brien, the representative of the Inner Party, says: "The Party seeks power entirely for its own sake. We are not interested in the good of the others; we are interested solely in power." The Stalinists and Nazis, he adds, had approached this view of power, but only in Oceania has all pretense to serving humanity—that is, all ideology—been discarded.

Social classes have at least one thing in common: an appetite for power. The bourgeoisie sought power, not primarily as an end in itself (whatever that vague phrase might mean), but in order to be free to expand its economic and social activity. The ruling class of the new totalitarian society, especially in Russia, is different, however, from previous ruling classes of our time: it does not think of political power as a means toward a nonpolitical end, as to some extent the bourgeoisie did; it looks upon political power as its essential end. For in a society where there is no private property the distinction between economic and political power becomes invisible.

So far this would seem to bear out Orwell's view. But if the ruling class of the totalitarian state does not conceive of political power as primarily a channel to tangible economic privileges, what *does* political power mean to it?

At least in the West, no modern ruling class has yet been able to dispense with ideology. All have felt an overwhelming need to rationalize their power, to proclaim some admirable objective as a justification for detestable acts. Nor is this mere slyness or hypocrisy; the rulers of a modern society can hardly survive without a certain degree of sincere belief in their own claims. They cling to ideology not merely to win and hold followers, but to give themselves psychological and moral assurance.

Can one imagine a twentieth century ruling class capable of discard-

ing these supports and acknowledging to itself the true nature of its
motives? I doubt it. Many Russian bureaucrats, in the relaxation of
private cynicism, may look upon their Marxist vocabulary as a useful
sham; but they must still cling to some vague assumption that somehow their political conduct rests upon ultimate sanctions. Were this
not so, the totalitarian ruling class would find it increasingly difficult,
perhaps impossible, to sustain its morale. It would go soft, it would
become corrupted in the obvious ways, it would lose the fanaticism
that is essential to its survival.

But ideology aside, there remains the enigma of totalitarian power.
And it *is* an enigma. Many writers have probed the origins of totalitarianism, the dynamics of its growth, the psychological basis of its appeal, the economic policies it employs when in power. But none of the
theorists who study totalitarianism can tell us very much about the
"ultimate purpose" of the Nazis or the Stalinists; in the end they come
up against the same difficulties as does Winston Smith in *1984* when he
says, "I understand HOW: I do not understand WHY."

Toward what end do the rulers of Oceania strive? They want power;
they want to enjoy the sense of exercising their power, which means to
test their ability to cause those below them to suffer. Yet the question
remains, why do they kill millions of people, why do they find pleasure
in torturing and humiliating people they know to be innocent? For
that matter, why did the Nazis and Stalinists? What is the image of the
world they desire, the vision by which they live?

I doubt that such questions can presently be answered, and it may be
that they are not even genuine problems. A movement in which terror
and irrationality play so great a role may finally have no goal beyond
terror and irrationality; to search for an ultimate end that can be significantly related to its immediate activity may itself be a rationalist
fallacy.

Orwell has been criticized by Isaac Deutscher for succumbing to a
"mysticism of cruelty" in explaining the behavior of Oceania's rulers,
which means, I suppose, that Orwell does not entirely accept any of the
usual socioeconomic theories about the aims of totalitarianism. It happens, however, that neither Mr. Deutscher nor anyone else has yet been
able to provide a satisfactory explanation for that systematic excess in
destroying human values which is a central trait of totalitarianism. I
do not say that the mystery need remain with us forever, since it is
possible that in time we shall be able to dissolve it into a series of
problems more easily manageable. Meanwhile, however, it seems absurd to attack a writer for acknowledging with rare honesty his sense of
helplessness before the "ultimate" meaning of totalitarianism—especially if that writer happens to have given us the most graphic vision

of totalitarianism that has yet been composed. For with *1984* we come to the heart of the matter, the whiteness of the whiteness.

V

Even while noting these possible objections to Orwell's book, I have been uneasily aware that they might well be irrelevant—as irrelevant, say, as the objection that no one can be so small as Swift's Lilliputians. What is more, it is extremely important to note that the world of 1984 is *not* totalitarianism as we know it, but totalitarianism after its world triumph. Strictly speaking, the society of Oceania might be called post-totalitarian. But I have let my objections stand simply because it may help the reader see Orwell's book somewhat more clearly if he considers their possible value and decides whether to accept or reject them.

1984 brings us to the end of the line. Beyond this—one feels or hopes —it is impossible to go. In Orwell's book the political themes of the novels that have been discussed in earlier chapters reach their final and terrible flowering, not perhaps in the way that writers like Dostoevsky or Conrad expected but in ways that establish a continuity of vision and value between the nineteenth and twentieth century political novelists.

There are some writers who live most significantly for their own age; they are writers who help redeem their time by forcing it to accept the truth about itself and thereby saving it, perhaps, from the truth about itself. Such writers, it is possible, will not survive their time, for what makes them so valuable and so endearing to their contemporaries— that mixture of desperate topicality and desperate tenderness—is not likely to be a quality conducive to the greatest art. But it should not matter to us, this possibility that in the future Silone or Orwell will not seem as important as they do for many people in our time. We know what they do for us, and we know that no other writers, including far greater ones, can do it.

In later generations *1984* may have little more than "historic interest." If the world of *1984* does come to pass, no one will read it except perhaps the rulers who will reflect upon its extraordinary prescience. If the world of *1984* does not come to pass, people may well feel that this book was merely a symptom of private disturbance, a nightmare. But we know better: we know that the nightmare is ours.

The Strangled Cry

by John Strachey

II. England

Arthur Koestler, if you meet him in the street, is Central Europe. George Orwell, walking down the road, was England—not, of course, the England of convention, of John Bull: just the contrary. He was one of the least bluff or hearty men who ever lived. He was another England: subtle, retired, but very sharp. He was the England of the major eccentrics, the major satirists. Lean and long of body, cadaverous, ravaged in face, with shining quixotic eyes, you might easily have taken him for one more English idealist crank. And so he nearly was. But in the end he became, for good and ill, far more than that. He was a major writer, and by means of his pen, he became one of the most effective men of his generation.

Animal Farm was his masterpiece. The contrast between it and *Darkness at Noon* could hardly be greater. At first glance, you might think that Orwell's little book hardly merited serious consideration in the context of world tragedy. *Animal Farm* is called on the title page 'A Fairy Story'; and so it is. (I met some children the other day who were greatly enjoying it without the slightest idea of what it was about; they were enjoying it not otherwise than generations of children have enjoyed *Gulliver*.) The farm which the animals capture by their revolution is a real English farm, in real English country. The book is downright pretty! How can one compare this elegant fancy with the unrelenting *reportage* of *Darkness at Noon*? And yet a dismissal of Orwell would be hasty.

The most famous passage in the book touches a theme which was to preoccupy Orwell for the rest of his life. After the revolution the ani-

From The Strangled Cry *by John Strachey (New York: William Sloane Associates, Inc., 1962), pp. 23–32. Copyright © 1962 by John Strachey. Reprinted by permission of William Morrow and Company, Inc.*

The selection reprinted here comprises the second part of a four-part essay on "reactionary literature"; in the other three parts Strachey discusses Arthur Koestler's Darkness at Noon, *Whittaker Chambers's* Witness, *and Boris Pasternak's* Dr. Zhivago.

mals had written up the seven commandments of "Animalism" upon the barn wall. The sixth was *"No animal shall kill any other animal,"* and the seventh was *"All animals are equal."* As time goes on, the animals notice, or half-notice, that some of these commandments don't look quite the same. For instance, after purges have begun the sixth commandment reads "No animal shall kill any other animal without cause." The words *"without cause"* had not been noticed before Finally, the animals find that all the commandments have disappeared except the last, and that this now reads *"All animals are equal, but some animals are more equal than others."*

Thus the subject which, together with physical torture, was to make Orwell hag-ridden for the rest of his life, had appeared. This is the theme of the falsification of the past. Orwell was obsessed with the conviction that in the last resort it was forgery, even more than violence, which could destroy human reason. Of course it must be forgery upon what the Communists call "a world-historical scale." But already, in 1945, when *Animal Farm* was published, Orwell had before him the elimination of Trotsky, the second figure of the Russian Revolution, from the historical record, almost as if he had never existed. Orwell was here reaching for what was to become his final conviction, namely that Communist rationalism, which sought to be rationalism pushed to its utmost conclusion, abruptly turned into its opposite of total irrationalism. He had had the hair-raising thought that an all-powerful government might have power over the past as well as over the present. If so, he was to show, human consciousness might be made to diverge permanently from objective reality into a land of subjective nightmare.

There is a sort of catch or trap set somewhere in the character of Orwell's type of Englishman. On the surface everything is easy and charming. The great English satirists write fables and fairy stories and the children love them. How can their fond countrymen compare such books with the furious polemics of continental political controversy? But look a little below the surface. A cold repugnance and despair is hidden in the pretty pages. After all the charm of Lilliput we encounter the Yahoos:

> . . . at three in the afternoon I got safe to my house at Rotherhithe. My wife and children received me with great surprise and joy, because they concluded me certainly dead; but I must freely confess the sight of them filled me only with hatred, disgust, and contempt . . . when I began to consider that by copulating with one of the Yahoo species I had become a parent of more, it struck me with the utmost shame, confusion, and horror. As soon as I entered the house my wife took me in her arms and kissed me; at which having not been used to the touch of that odious animal for so many years, I fell into a swoon for almost an hour.

The great repugnance was in Orwell too. And before his death it was to find overt expression.

Orwell's second major political work was less perfect than *Animal Farm* just because it was so much more overt. Nevertheless *Nineteen Eighty-Four* is a formidable book and it has been immensely influential. Orwell lent his powerful, detailed, concrete imagination to the task of describing a nightmare, in order, if possible, which he very much doubted, to avert it. The result is the most intolerable of all the pessimistic, inverted, Utopias. The condition of England in *Nineteen Eighty-Four* has become, down to the minutest detail, everything which Orwell most abominated and which most terrified him.

The main theme of the book is thought-control in general and control over the past in particular. In this field the particularity of Orwell's imagination is remarkable. At the first level, thought-control is exercised by two-way television sets in every room, by means of which the "Thought Police" can see and listen to, as well as, if they like, be seen by, every citizen at any time, day or night. At the next level the government is introducing a new language called *"Newspeak,"* the object of which is nothing less than to make it impossible to express thoughts unwelcome to the authorities. The substitution of "Newspeak" for "Oldspeak" (or present-day English) is designed to effect nothing less than the destruction of human reason by linguistic means. I do not know if any of the contemporary school of linguistic philosophers have made a study of Orwell in this respect. To the layman his *tour de force* of imagination is extremely effective, producing a genuine realisation of the extent to which, precisely, "language, truth, and logic" are interdependent. A prime object of Newspeak is so drastically to cut down the vocabulary that the expression of heretical ideas, and with a few simple exceptions, ideas at all, becomes impossible.

> All words grouping themselves round the concepts of liberty and equality, for instance, were contained in the single word *"Crimethink,"* while all words grouping themselves round the concept of objectivity and rationalism were contained in the single word *"Oldthink."*

The book has a detailed and learned linguistic Appendix on the problems presented by this enterprise. This Appendix is in many respects much more alarming than the melodrama of the latter part of the book. Moreover, more than the acquisition of the new language is required for the governors themselves, the members of the Inner Party. They must be provided with a philosophy. This need is met by *doublethink,* a philosophy based on a version of extreme subjectivism—indeed it is solipsism—which enables its practitioners sincerely to believe a proposition at one level and its opposite at a deeper level.

The horror of all this is focused for Winston Smith, Orwell's hero, in the party's procedure and apparatus for altering the past. When, for example, there is a "diplomatic revolution," and Oceania, the dictatorship of which England (now called Airstrip One) is a part, changes sides in the permanent world war which is being waged, so that she is now fighting, say, Eurasia and is allied with Eastasia, the party at once blots out all record of the fact that up till then she has been fighting Eastasia and been allied to Eurasia. Any verbal allusion to or hint of the change is punished by instant death. Every file copy of every newspaper is suitably re-written and re-printed. Every record of every speech is amended. (Winston Smith is professionally employed by the Ministry of Truth on this quite skilled re-write job.) All other records are systematically destroyed by being dropped into great furnaces, down the "memory holes" with which the Ministry is equipped. The same procedure is used when there is occasion to shoot leading members of the Inner Party; a new incriminating past, amply documented from contemporary records, is manufactured for them, and all record of their actual past is eliminated. Smith is especially fascinated and terrified by this past-control procedure. In the end, under torture, his "Gletkin" (O'Brien) explains to him that to a man more adequately educated in *doublethink* than he is, the past really is altered. For all records, and in a little while all consciousness, of the old past are destroyed, and records and consciousness of a new past are provided. Therefore, as reality is wholly subjective, there is no problem. The party has power over the past also.

In *Nineteen Eighty-Four* the party has not yet achieved its objective of moulding human nature in a wholly suitable way. Members of the Outer Party are still subject to regrettable lapses, and a tense struggle by all means, from education, spying, torture, and shooting, has to be waged to keep them in line. Above all, personal private life has to be eliminated to the maximum possible extent.

Winston Smith, though in his thoughts alone, has begun to deviate. He knows that such deviations, even if they remain forever unspoken, must lead to his death under torture; but he cannot, or will not, wholly control his thoughts. His downfall is simple and natural. The girls of the Outer Party are subjected to an intensely puritanical education, designed to make them incapable of any pleasure in the sexual act. Marital intercourse is permitted, but only so long as it is joyless. It is known as "our weekly party duty"; but all other sexual intercourse is punishable by death. Smith has noticed a girl who seems a particularly strident and horrible example of the "party norm." She screams particularly loudly in the "hate periods," volunteers for even more of the party work than is necessary, and appears odiously athletic, puri-

tanical, and conformist. To his dismay this girl seems to be eyeing him.
Has she sensed his deviations? He keeps running across her, too often
for it to be chance. She is probably an agent of the Thought Police.
He thinks he is done for. Then she slips a scrap of paper into his hand.
He cannot at once look at it.

> Whatever was written on the paper, it must have some kind of po-
> litical meaning. So far as he could see there were two possibilities. One,
> much the more likely, was that the girl was an agent of the Thought
> Police, just as he had feared. He did not know why the Thought Police
> should choose to deliver their messages in such a fashion, but perhaps
> they had their reasons. The thing that was written on the paper might
> be a threat, a summons, an order to commit suicide, a trap of some de-
> scription. But there was another, wilder possibility that kept raising its
> head, though he tried vainly to suppress it. This was, that the message did
> not come from the Thought Police at all, but from some kind of under-
> ground organisation.

At the first safe moment, he unrolls the screwed-up paper. On it are
written the three words:

I LOVE YOU

The rest of the book is largely concerned with the resultant love-
affair between Smith and Julia, and the innate subversiveness of love
is well displayed. Here is a private passion, uncontrolled and unregu-
lated by the party, a passion strong enough to make people act independently and spontaneously. No wonder the party sees the necessity
of stamping it out.

Julia turns out to be by no means a romantic revolutionary, nor yet
an intellectual. She just wants some hearty sex, normally mingled with
tender emotion. Somehow she has preserved her power of natural joy
against the conditioning of the party. She has secretly copulated with
quite a few Outer Party members already. She simply wants Winston
Smith as her man. But it is precisely this assertion of the human norm
which must lead, Orwell demonstrates (he never asserts), to revolt
against the party norm. Winston and Julia begin, with infinite difficulty and circumspection, to create a secret private life for themselves.
The preservation of Julia's sexual normality has led her to regard the
whole party ideology as tosh. This is already intolerable because,
though in Julia it does not even prompt her to any kind of action, in
an intellectual like Winston Smith it leads directly to dreams of revolt.

So far *Nineteen Eighty-Four* is magnificently achieved. But from the
moment when Winston and Julia are, inevitably, caught and their in-
terrogation and torture begins, the book deteriorates. It is not, to be
sure, that Orwell's powers of imagination fail. On the contrary, the

fanatical ingenuity with which both intellectual and physical tortures are described cannot be exaggerated. But the fact is that the subject of physical torture, though it was clearly another of his obsessions, was not one with which Orwell was equipped to deal. He had never been tortured, any more than most of the rest of us have been. And those who have no personal experience of this matter may be presumed to know nothing whatever about it.

Be that as it may, Orwell's preoccupation with torture and terror gives his book the agonised and frenzied note—the note of the strangled cry—which characterises this literature as a whole. In Orwell's case alone the cause of his frenzy is largely subjective. Both Koestler and Pasternak's actual manuscripts had to be smuggled away from authorities disposed to suppress them. Their authors were in danger of their lives from those authorities. Chambers also wrote his book in an atmosphere of seething melodrama, of papers hidden in pumpkins, of the Communist underground, of FBI agents and the Hiss case. Orwell wrote *Nineteen Eighty-Four* in the relative stability of post-war Britain. What gives it its frenzy is probably that it is the work of a dying man: for when Orwell wrote it he was already in an advanced stage of tuberculosis.

The practical influence of *Nineteen Eighty-Four* (and it was appreciable) was, in Britain, reactionary in the narrow political sense of that term. Many of those who for one reason or another felt that their interests were threatened by the British Labour Government, which was in its period of office when the book was published, managed to persuade themselves that the British brand of democratic socialism was taking the country along the road to *Nineteen Eighty-Four*. That almost pedantically libertarian government (which, for instance, made it possible, for the first time in British history for a subject to sue the government) was solemnly arraigned as intending, or at any rate tending, to take us all into the Orwellian nightmare. But of course authors cannot be held responsible for the wilder distortions of their meaning which some readers will inevitably make. In fact it has been the fairly thorough overhaul of the British system, mainly (though by no means exclusively) carried out by the Labour Government, which has given a vigorous new lease of life to British democratic and libertarian institutions. This is an example of the tendency of this whole literature to damage the very forces which, by maintaining a tolerable social balance, can avert all that these writers so desperately, and so justly, fear.

On the central issue posed in these pages, namely the issue of the contemporary retreat from rationalism as a whole, *Nineteen Eighty-Four* is significant in another way. The European, the American, and even perhaps the Russian, authors whose works we are discussing, all consider, we shall find, that Communism is the culmination of the rationalist tradition. In this sense they consider that Communism *is* rationalism in its contemporary form. Hence when they depict what they consider to be the ghastly consequences of Communism and cry for its repudiation, they must perforce repudiate rationalism also. And to a varying degree this is what each of them does. Koestler considers that reason has run amuck: that now it must be limited by the "Oceanic sense," which is his name for mystical experience. Chambers forthrightly declares that there is no alternative to Communism except an acceptance of the supernatural: that no one who does not accept one form or other of supernaturalism has really broken with Communism. Pasternak's message is, it is true, far more subtle. Nevertheless he devotes his masterpiece to showing how little those sides of life which, he considers, can alone be dealt with rationally, matter as compared with those deeper elements in the human condition which can only be handled by superrational methods.

Orwell, the Englishman, alone implies an opposite view. In *Nineteen Eighty-Four* Communism itself, now indistinguishable from Fascism, is depicted as patently irrational. It has lost almost all touch with objective reality and pursues psychopathic social objectives. Moreover, Orwell is here, of course, merely extrapolating into the year 1984 those tendencies of Communism which, he considered, were only too apparent in 1949. The lesson of his book is *not* that the catastrophe which Communism has suffered proves that reason carried to its logical conclusion leads to horror; that consequently we must retreat from reason into some form of mysticism or supernaturalism. On the contrary, what Orwell is saying is that the catastrophe of our times occurred precisely because the Communists (and, of course, still more the Fascists) deserted reason. He is saying that the Communists, without being aware of it, have lost touch with reality: that their doctrine has become, precisely, a mysticism, an authoritarian revelation.

Orwell nowhere argues all this. He nowhere makes it clear that he is denouncing both Fascism and Communism from a rational standpoint. It would not have occurred to him to do any such thing. His rationalism is of the rough-and-ready, highly empirical, English kind. He is undidactic, untheoretical. But nowhere, equally, does he suggest the alternative of mysticism or supernaturalism. Indeed his whole satire, in both books, is directed to demonstrating that once criticism has been suppressed, a society must inevitably come to depend upon authority, revelation, and mystery. His whole message is epigrammatically contained in his famous aphorism that the original proposition that *"all animals are equal"* will, in the absence of freedom to dissent, inevitably receive the addendum *"but some animals are more equal than others.*" In other words, without the liberty of prophesying, the subtleties of the dialectic will degenerate into the obscenities of *doublethink.* For him it is not that the Communists have discredited reason by pushing it to its logical conclusion. On the contrary, it is that they have betrayed reason by abandoning its living empirical methodology for an unchanging revelation. His whole satire was an exposure of the consequences of pathological unreason. Therefore, though he did not say anything, or perhaps even think anything, about it, his books are at bottom a defence, all the more unquestioning for being tacit, of the assumptions of traditional English empiricism.

If Orwell had been a more systematic thinker he might perhaps have fused his brilliant linguistic insights with his general political outlook to form a social philosophy of a particularly concrete and applied character. He might have sorted out for us the question of why and how reason may at a certain point tumble over into "rationalism," in the narrow, rigid, and dogmatic sense of that word: into a kind of "rationalism" which is fully as authoritarian as the tenets of a revealed religion. He might have given social empiricism a firmer basis, and at the same time shown us how to do justice to those personal, aesthetic, and religious values about which we can as yet say so little—except that we can all now see that their neglect is fatal. I do not know whether, if he had lived, Orwell might have attempted something of the sort. This at least is the direction in which his work pointed. . . .

Introduction to *1984*

by Stephen Spender

George Orwell's *1984* has become a byword like *Gulliver's Travels, Robinson Crusoe, The Castle* and *Brave New World*. Such books have in common certain ideas encapsuled in phrases—catchwords even—which have entered into our thinking about the human situation. The conditions their writers caricature may be in the present or future, they may be narrowly economic or social, or they may—as with Swift—be largely concerned with our physiological being. But reading them one feels that the trap of time in which human individuals live has been described even though the general picture be "exaggerated."

Utopias, or counter-Utopias, are chimeras: made up of ideas drawn from many sources and put together in combinations that produce Yahoos, Man Friday, Musical Banks, Double-Think and Newspeak—to mention only a few.

Today we are particularly aware of one category of Future-haunted writing—Science Fiction. In trying to "place" Orwell's *1984* it is important to distinguish it from most scientific counter-Utopias.

It seems to me that *1984* is closer to Samuel Butler's *Erewhon* than to Kafka or Wells or Huxley, though it contains scraps of scientific prophecy. There is also, not only in the gritty writing, but in the literalness of its invented world, and in the commonsense yet eccentric Englishness of the view of "the proles," something of Defoe.

1984 has indeed qualities which are distributed among several categories. There are elements of science fiction, but still more of Defoe and Swift, who are both so concerned with meticulous accounts of worlds seen in detailed miniature. Orwell's novel seems to have the same kind of relation to the twentieth century as Samuel Butler's *Erewhon* does to the nineteenth. Butler though is more preoccupied with guying Darwin's theory of evolution than with seriously suggesting that the machine might take over from human beings. Orwell is

"Introduction" to 1984 *by Stephen Spender (London: Heinemann Educational Books Ltd, 1965 [Modern Novel Series]), pp. vii–xxi. Copyright © 1965 by Stephen Spender. Reprinted by permission of Heinemann Educational Books Ltd.*

describing a society in which, the more closely we look at it, the more clearly we see that a machinery of indoctrinated ideology, perpetual war, police terror and brain-washing has taken over. The society of *1984* is machine-fed not on petroleum but on ideology. Both the machine and the ideology are dehumanized.

There was a rumour that Orwell wished to call his novel, *1948,* but was dissuaded from doing so because his publishers felt the title exaggerated. True or not, this emphasizes Orwell's own sense of closeness to the situation he was describing. A paragraph in an essay he wrote about Arthur Koestler shows he felt that modern circumstances made detachment impossible. He compares the problem Koestler had in writing *The Gladiators* (a historical novel about the rebel Roman slave Spartacus) with that of Flaubert writing *Salammbo,* in the nineteenth century:

> Flaubert could think himself into the stony cruelty of antiquity, because in the mid-nineteenth century one still had peace of mind. One had time to travel in the past. Nowadays the present and the future are too terrifying to be escaped from, and if one bothers with history it is in order to find modern meanings there.

A good deal of *1984* is satiric, but, owing to the proximity of terror, and the lack of "peace of mind," the novel lacks the detachment of a Swift. The writing is not witty, barbed, ironic. Extremely close to its object and drawn, as it were, in black ink or charcoal, Orwell's method is serious caricature. Orwell indeed would not want to evade the danger of the work being regarded as symptomatic of the conditions from which it derives. He detests the world of 1984 (or 1948?); he does not pretend to be detached from it. It is a world almost drained of the values of living. This aridity is reflected in the style, which though correct and sometimes forceful has more of machine-like drive than exuberance and vitality. The evoked symbols of the recollected past (the gesture with which a woman flings aside her dress, the transparent world enclosed in a glass paper-weight, the name of Shakespeare), are flash-backs, cinematic clichés like the love-scenes between his "hero" and "heroine" Winston Smith and Julia.

The world of *1984* is almost entirely secular and almost entirely contemporary, shut off from any past earlier than Edwardian England. God does not enter in through any chink of it, and sex is a corruption without pagan celebration. Orwell does not, like Swift, have a theology which sets part of him above the humanity he finds disgusting. Nor like Kafka (in *The Trial, The Castle*—even *The Penal Colony*) does he point to some authority which gives mystery to the folly and wrongness of human behaviour. He is neither orthodoxly religious nor a mystic. Civilized values in *1984* resemble survivals of vestigial physical organs—the tonsils or the appendix. Their significance is precisely that they are survivals, nostalgically useless in a world dominated by the mechanical means serving the depersonalized ends of power.

In the passage quoted above about Koestler, Orwell writes that today there is not time to travel in the past. In a sense he has no time to travel in the future either: or not, that is, into any future which is different, in the sense of resulting from the exercise of human freedom, from the present. The nightmare of Orwell's future—a boot stamped forever into a human face—is that it is no future. It is the prison of the perpetuated present in which the only things which change are technological advances, combined with the manœuvres of political groups worshipping their own power, making the present in which there is no human freedom, ever more inescapable. The future projected by power, war, propaganda, brain-washing, espionage and police terror, all continuously "improved" by machinery is *Plus ça change plus c'est la même chose* forever writ larger and larger on a static history. That is all.

Orwell's nightmare derives from a vision of such a stasis already implicit in the "pink decade" of the 1930's. This was when Hitler established the German Third Reich which was supposed to last a thousand years, destroyed all opposition in Germany, branded the Jews and many others as sexual inferiors, converted many of those religious and intellectuals who were originally his opponents by the moral force of the power he exercised, and demonstrated that propaganda machinery run by men who boasted that the biggest lie could deceive more people more effectively than a small one, could, by the enlistment of all the organs of publicity into its service, nevertheless deceive people.

Even more impressive than Hitler, though, was Stalin. Stalin, with his purges in which ideological and convinced communists were made to confess that they were traitors, his switches of policy which could overnight claim an enemy as an ally, or denounce an ally as an enemy, above all by the use to which he put the argument that whatever Stalin did was "on the side of history," and whatever any opponent did irrelevant or reactionary, showed how modern history could become completely identified with the decisions of a central committee carrying out a scientifically conceived policy and under the direction of one man.

Some of Stalin's most ardent supporters outside Russia were intellectuals professing to defend freedom. Orwell's view of the future was influenced by consideration of the support given to one kind of totalitarian system (Stalinism) by European intellectuals when it was opposed by another totalitarian system (Hitlerism). If the intellectuals in the democracies could defend Stalin's purges, then what would happen if—as Orwell thought by no means unlikely—their own governments became dictatorships? There seemed to Orwell a likelihood that a great part of the world would go either Communist or Fascist. And if this did not happen in an obvious sense, nevertheless the combination of the machinery of centralized power, combined with the betrayal of standards of objective truth of the intellectuals, would result in the triumph of the means of power over the ends of human freedom.

In *Homage to Catalonia*, Orwell (who fought on the Catalan Front in the Spanish Civil War as an anarchist) shows how the Spanish Republic, fighting against one kind of totalitarianism, fell more and more under the control of another. The liquidation by the Republican forces of the anarchist-Trotskyite P.O.U.M. organization was to him the demonstration of this. That most leftist intellectuals who supported the Spanish Republic did not have a word to say in defence of the P.O.U.M. increased Orwell's contempt for them. Out of his own experience in the 1930's he came to the conclusion that the only class in which there may linger hope for the future of human freedom is the "proles," because they care for concrete things and are unaffected by ideology.

Orwell has been attacked because *1984* offers so little hope for the future. We have been told that in depicting so much despair he was influenced by feelings about his own last illness, or by his unhappiness as a boy at his preparatory school described in that passionately indignant autobiographical essay, *Such Were the Joys*. He has been accused of taking over the ideas of an earlier writer and of representing it without acknowledgement as his own. Isaac Deutscher suggests that Orwell's borrowings from Zamyatin's *We* amount almost (though Deutscher stops short of the term) to plagiarism. Yet whatever Orwell's debt to Zamyatin (I do not believe it is as great as Deutscher makes out), *1984* is vastly more significant than *We*.

To reproach Orwell for being too pessimistic is misleading. His novel sets out reasonably to demonstrate despair, it is about the possibility of all the processes of a totally politicized world becoming canalized into the dehumanized functionings of the State; of love and joy becoming gestures at best ineffectual and at worst subversive.

One must ask whether *1984* describes conditions that are today potential, not whether it is too depressing or subjective. If Orwell's vision expresses a real potentiality, then to ask for it to be transformed by love or hope or joy is like asking Dante to put more joy in the picture which is his *Inferno*. The strength of *1984* is the strength with which Orwell brings forward into consciousness a fear that in the not too remote future all independent personal values may become replaced by social conditioning, each individual become in his behaviour and in his innermost thinking and feeling the projection of an ideology imposed by some central authority. This is, I have suggested, primarily a twentieth-century extension of a modern atavistic fear already expressed by Samuel Butler in the late nineteenth century, the fear of the machine: though Orwell is concerned not so much with rocket atom bombs, telecasters, and other mechanical inventions, as with ideologies, systems of thinking, methods of persuasion, propaganda. In the hands of Big Brother, these might be called mind-machines. They enslave men's thinking to such an extent that the only hope for the future will lie in the lives of those who do not think, but merely work and play—"the proles." Yet his starting-point remains the Sorcerer's Apprentice, as the concluding paragraph of the essay *Freedom and Happiness* in which he discusses Zamyatin's *We* shows. *We* (he writes) is "in effect a study of the Machine, the genie that man has thoughtlessly let out of its bottle and cannot put back again."

So in *1984* Orwell takes up the fear that man can use machinery in order to condition his own consciousness—make of himself a machine not at the service of other machines but of a centralized controlling ideology beyond which lies only mystique of power. In the concluding scene, when O'Brien convinces Winston Smith of the truth of the propositions "Freedom is Slavery," "Two and Two make Five," and when he finally forces him to love Big Brother, it is the electric charge through his physical nerves, controlled by the dials on the machine operated by O'Brien, which causes Winston to submit. But there are indications enough that this current has at some time flowed through O'Brien himself—the victim of the ideology which makes him a tyrant. When O'Brien causes the television to project before Winston Smith's eyes his face transformed by torture to "a forlorn, jailbird's face with a nobbly forehead running back into a bald scalp, a crooked nose and battered-looking cheekbones," O'Brien comments "You have thought sometimes, that my face—the face of a member of the Inner Party— looks old and worn."

The victimization of Winston Smith by the Inner Party Member— himself a victim of Big Brother—whose very existence is in doubt—is made possible by the total mobilization of all the surrounding social forces against the individual. It is the atomization of individual consciousness by the Party Leaders whose minds and lives (apart from some dubious privileges which they enjoy) have become completely identified with theory and whose actions are dictated by an abstract necessity.

The operation of political philosophy upon individual human beings is of course impossible without a machinery, just as the smashing of the atom is impossible without a reactor. With before him the example of concentration camps, the Russian Trials and purges, and the betrayal he called the Sin of the European intelligentsia—the intellectuals supporting one kind of a totalitarian regime against another—Orwell conceived of a world in which authority would become a reactor smashing human atoms. Here he borrowed extensively from the Marxist theory of imperialist wars, with empires fighting one another to extend their own markets while at the same time they are concerned to keep down the proletariat. The three empires into which his world is divided fight one another to obtain cheap labour, competition for which prevents them coming to agreement which would lead to a single world dictatorship united in enslaving the masses. No side aims at complete victory over the other, for this might lead to excessive destruction. Moreover, all three sides secretly agree in the secondary aim of Big Brother which is the enslavement of the masses, the "proles."

In all this, Orwell assumed that the future would consist of the politics of the time at which he was writing, writ large. He foresaw in effect the extension of symptoms produced during the Second World War. He thought that Western and Eastern allies would turn against one another. Each unit would become a gigantic police state, with concentration camps, rationing and controls.

As we approach the real 1984, it seems improbable that—in the West at all events—there will be a society of deliberately organized poverty. Moreover, with hydrogen and perhaps also cobalt bomb skeletons in the cupboard, we feel pretty sure that a *1984*-type war, so far from procrastinating endlessly, would mean the end of human life. Today we cannot conceive of world war going on indefinitely, yet Orwell's transparent wrongness in some respects does not disqualify his main idea that the future of centralized government lies in thought control. If his cruder suggestions seem improbable, the more detailed ones of citizens spied on by telescreens, living in rooms bugged by microphones, have already in several countries been fulfilled. In addition to these negative instruments there is also the development of positive psychological influences: advertising (perhaps subliminal), drugs and other means of transforming the environment into an atmosphere which spies, persuades, blandly terrorizes. Orwell anticipates universal awareness of violent terror. What today we may fear is our brains being washed by persuasions of which we are scarcely conscious, conditioning so subtle that among the conditioning factors we must count an illusion of freedom. There are behind the Iron Curtain, countries today where the freedom of artists and writers has been reduced to that of prisoners free to scrawl obscenities on their prison walls. And the fact that such a caricature of freedom exists helps advertise the government, which has no fear of a confined and rigorously supervised "self-expression."

So Orwell read the future into the political instruments and ideologies of the 1930's. He was hypnotized almost by the idea that the political will could translate all mental activities, all personal psychology into its instruments. That it would do this simply was "the future," was in effect *1984*. Newspeak, Double-Think, the arguments of O'Brien, the propaganda of Big Brother, the politics of the Inner Party, are simply Orwell reading the 1930's writing on the wall, and translating its jargon into his own plain language. He did not really have to read *We* to discover the idiom of his counter-Utopia, he need only have read Communist party propaganda, or the speeches of Goebbels, or examined documentary evidence such as this, from the mouth of Albert Speer, at the Nuremberg trials:

> The telephone, the teleprinter and the wireless made it possible for orders from the highest levels to be given direct to the lowest levels, where, on account of the absolute authority behind them, they were carried out uncritically; or they brought it about that numerous offices and command centres were directly connected with the supreme leadership from which they received their sinister orders without any intermediary; or they resulted in a widespread surveillance of the citizen; or in a high degree of secrecy surrounding criminal happenings. To the outside observer this governmental apparatus may have resembled the apparently chaotic confusion of lines at a telephone exchange, but like the latter it could be controlled and operated from one central source. Former dictatorships need collaborators of high quality even in lower levels of leaderships, men who could think and act independently. In an era of modern technique an authoritarian system can do without this. The means of communication alone permit it to mechanize the work of subordinate leadership. As a consequence a new type develops: the uncritical recipient of orders.

The will at the centre which gives the orders also invents the reality of the State. There is in the initial stages, or according to an older manner of thinking, a divorce between reality invented by a centralized will in control of the environment and truth—the truth of facts such as that twice two are four, perceived by other minds than the controlling mind. But finally this truth itself falls into doubt where it has no place within the reality created by total politics, the picture of history invented by the ideologists, the myth becomes the material environment. In the 1930's Orwell saw Stalin inventing the reality which was the "necessary" means used by the dictatorship. Stalin's opponents and victims were "liquidated"; that is to say they were treated as material to be disposed of like the rock that might impede the cutting of a canal or a tunnel. They and all they stood for were dismissed as though they had never existed (unless they survived in memory as useful warnings) because they stood in the way of the path of a history in which the ends justified the means. And essentially the "crime" of the victims of the Nazis was that, in Hitler's eyes, they were simply not to be regarded as human beings. Therefore they had to be vaporized, they were non-human material, like the ground that is dug up and thrown away to make a trench.

The interpretation of the past by the ideologists meant its absorption as prophecies, dreams, myths, reachings towards the present, within the reality which would remain forever the present. Thus Marxists could give the christianity of antiquity their blessing because it could be regarded not as a religion but as the symbolic projection of an idea-system of slaves, rebelling against their masters. It could be "historically" justified by a history that knew better. Shakespeare was approved of because he could be said to express the individualism which was an advance on feudalism, which was in turn to be superseded by the middle classes, which in turn would finally be superseded by the victorious proletariat. The dictatorship of the proletariat would not be superseded, because it was the final goal of history.

Thus the truths of the past expressed in philosophies, religions, myths, poetry, and art, were seen to be stages of myth ready to be assumed into the reality and final stage of conscious self-perpetuating truth which was the totally politicized present. The future also was enclosed within the present, because the interpretation of every human activity into terms of an authoritarian political consciousness was held to be the final stage of the development of history. It embodied the victory of the proletariat, or of the superior race, in the will of the central committee of the party. The prison in the minds of the dictators which proliferated into so many real prisons where opponents were broken or liquidated, was simply the present moment of the politically conscious will, into which the whole of the past had been absorbed and which projected its philosophy of will and action into the whole of the future.

To argue (as does Mr. Deutscher) that George Orwell never mastered Marxism, makes no difference to the fact that in practice (that is to say, in the wills of Stalin and Hitler) the dictators foreshadowed in their sayings and their acts a future which was the perpetuation of their system. The history of that period is a few haunting clichés: "freedom is the recognition of necessity," "the ends justify the means," "the dictatorship of the proletariat," "the super-race," and Hitler's prophecy of the rule of his Party that would last a thousand years.

Orwell has been accused of being unable to provide any explanation of the politics of *1984* except a mystique of power. Winston Smith understands *how* the system works, he does not understand *why*. When O'Brien mockingly asks him *why,* he can only think of answers that are conventional Party propaganda:

> He knew in advance what O'Brien would say:
> "That the party did not seek power for its own ends, but only for the good of the majority. That it sought power because men in the mass were frail, cowardly creatures who could not endure the truth, and must be ruled over and systematically deceived by others who were stronger than themselves."

O'Brien "reads" these thoughts on Winston Smith's face, and answers him:

> The Party seeks power only for its own sake. We are not interested in the good of others; we are interested only in power. . . . Power is not a means, it is an end. One does not establish a dictatorship in order to safeguard a revolution; one makes the revolution in order to establish the dictatorship. The object of torture is torture. The object of power is power. Now do you begin to understand me?

This answer has been criticized because it is not a political answer. After all (it is pointed out), even if the purges got out of hand and became to some extent an expression of the personality of the tyrant, Stalin can be explained very largely in terms of politics, Hitler had motivations which were of forces not just Hitler.

What Orwell saw was that when the forces exercised by political authorities become sufficiently powerful they lead back to human nature. The makers of revolutions who trample over human rights and have no regard for individuals can be analysed firstly perhaps as the expression of historic forces swept to power by historic injustices. They are the results of a "revolutionary situation"—but once established in power they may be analysed as the kind of people who attained power because they combined revolutionary zeal for a cause with indifference to human suffering. They did not hear the child's cry or watch the fall of a sparrow, at first because they identified themselves with a cause, but at last because they were ruthless, indifferent, cruel. Absolute power which seems the result perhaps of an absolute objectivity comes out, when it is achieved, as the realization of subjective human character, perhaps even as a result of man's thirst for what is called "the absolute"—absolute control of absolute solutions. Enjoyment of power for its own sake is as much as a man will ever taste of power, and perhaps in this lies the thirst for power. And although this may not, to a political philosopher, be apparent, it is so in the lives of the leaders who put ideologies into action. The novelist who translates public behaviour back into the psychology and individual characters has something to say to us.

A political philosopher is someone who interprets multifold minute particulars of human beings into general principles of social motivation. As such, of course, he is necessary, and modern industrial societies which were not organized along general lines and according to general principles would be disorganized starving multitudes. Nevertheless it is the task of a novelist to interpret ideology back into human psychology, to explain the ideologists and those who execute their ideas, to see them as human beings disposed to embrace these ideas for reasons similar to those which explain the character of Pierre Bezukov or Lucien de Rubempré or Robinson Crusoe.

The answer to *how* in *1984* is analysis and description of the machinery; but the answer to *why* leads away from politics back into human nature. The criticism which might be made of Orwell's novel is that he does not follow this thread far enough, for somewhere it must lead back into a past which exists independently of the present, into the religious and imaginative aspects of human character.

In *1984,* the representatives of historic human qualities, who to some extent stand outside the machinery of the continuously present moment, are Winston Smith and, to a lesser extent, Julia. I use the term "representatives" advisedly, because that is what Winston and Julia have to be. They can no more be developed characters than can Gulliver, Robinson Crusoe, or the hero of *Erewhon Revisited.* Their function is to answer the question in the mind of the reader, "How could I fit into such a world?"—a world which by definition prevents the full development of a novelistic "character." What one might complain of in Winston Smith is that he has too much the limitations of Orwell himself, his creator. He represents a surviving decency, and a rather desperate awareness of his own body, but in no respect the mystery of things. He is in fact a stereotype of the 1930's, *l'homme moyen sensuel,* the average man sensually aware of his humanity, like the hero in Ionesco's play, who because of his average humanness just avoids becoming, as all his neighbours do become, a rhinoceros.

One may suspect that in making Winston Smith love Big Brother— even more than in making him see that two and two do add up to five (as they well may do!)—Orwell overloads the case against humanity. In Auschwitz and Buchenwald, although the majority were dehumanized, a few were not. They rejected Big Brother. And if they had become convinced that the Concentration Camp was humanity they would have found faith in something not human.

Orwell is concerned then with limited truth, the truth of man entirely conditioned by and within politics, within society. He has little interest in seeking for ultimate truth, and this prevents his novel being an affirmation of man's spirit. But it may be argued that if he had followed a thread which leads outside the world of total conditioning, the warning of *1984* would have been less effective.

Orwell perhaps lacked poetry, but, looking at our modern world of ideologies and wars, he echoes the message of Wilfred Owen, the greatest poet of the First World War: "All a poet can do today is to warn." *1984* remains, by and large, a necessary warning.

The Road to *1984*

by George Kateb

I

In an extremely hostile essay, published in 1956 on the occasion of the American printing of Orwell's early novel, *Keep the Aspidistra Flying*, the critic Anthony West said that "only the existence of a hidden wound can account for such a remorseless pessimism." The pessimism to which West referred was that of the world of *1984*, although West found that the whole body of Orwell's writings—including his first novels—was pessimistic through and through. For West, that pessimism was largely inauthentic. Orwell's despair over poverty, for example, is understood by West to be mostly "the mood of a man who feels inadequate and despised because he is not rich." Orwell's indictment of his early school years in the essay "Such, Such Were the Joys," leads West to remark that "what Orwell represents as an apparatus designed to cripple him was in actuality an attempt to give boys like him a chance to win the best possible start in life." West does not even hesitate to say that Orwell felt "cheated" by the refusal of the British to surrender to the Nazis: his morbidity could have been satisfied only by a colossal disaster. And in his chagrin, Orwell, says West, "consoled himself by constructing a fantasy of universal ruin." [1] The upshot is that the real way of coming to terms with *1984* is to assume its worthlessness except as a contribution to the psychopathology of George Orwell, as that work of Orwell's which, more than any other, expressed the fundamental sickness of the man.

West is not the only writer to find the pessimism of *1984* excessive, not warranted by even the worst events of modern times, and to suggest that some argument *ad hominem* could alone explain the blackness of Orwell's last book. To leave aside all that may be exag-

"*The Road to* 1984" *by George Kateb. From* The Political Science Quarterly 81 *(December 1966): 564–80. Reprinted by permission of the publisher.*

[1] Anthony West, "George Orwell," reprinted in West's *Principles and Persuasions* (New York, 1957), pp. 166, 167, 171, 176.

gerated in the rest of Orwell's work, *1984* does seem to go too far, so far as to have earned for itself a wide reputation for implausibility. Isaac Deutscher, among others, has attributed to the book "the mysticism of cruelty." But where West obviously delights in his nastiness toward Orwell, and offers little clarification and no sympathy, Deutscher tries to account for Orwell's extremism. Deutscher thinks that Orwell's illness doubtless played some part in determining him to write such a fearful book. "But," says Deutscher, "the main explanation of the inner logic of Orwell's disillusionment and pessimism lies not in the writer's death agonies, but in the experience and the thought of the living man and in his convulsive reaction from his defeated rationalism." The point is that even on the most generous estimation of Orwell's character, the conclusion is inescapable that some serious personal shortcoming, rather than the force of historical events, produced a book like *1984*. The shortcoming is intellectual in nature: "for at heart," says Deutscher, "Orwell was a simple-minded anarchist and, in his eyes, any political movement forfeited its *raison d'être* the moment it acquired a *raison d'état*." [2] A hatred of politics came to dominate Orwell in the last years of his life; and from such hatred, an immature and unacceptable view of politics had to result. Political wisdom presupposes acceptance of historical necessities.

Now it is undeniable that one's first response to *1984* will most likely be incredulity. Above all, the motives of the Inner Party seem altogether out of the realm of likelihood. To attribute love of power to political men is commonplace; to insist that this love is almost always present among political men, and often takes malevolent forms, could hardly meet with disagreement. But Orwell does go beyond that; he goes beyond hard-headed realism, beyond cynicism, also well beyond the normal liberal dread of men in power. He goes beyond Tacitus, Machiavelli, Hobbes, and Nietzsche in their speculation on the degrees and kinds of pleasure men can take in wielding power. O'Brien, member of the Inner Party, and the pursuer and tormentor of Winston, instructs Winston on the psychology of the men at the top:

> The Party seeks power entirely for its own sake. We are not interested in the good of others; we are interested solely in power. Not wealth or luxury or long life or happiness; only power, pure power. . . . Power is power over human beings. . . . Unless he is suffering, how can you be sure that he is obeying your will and not his own? Power is in inflicting pain and humiliation. Power is in tearing human minds to pieces and putting them together again in new shapes of your own choosing. . . .

[2] Isaac Deutscher, " '1984'—The Mysticism of Cruelty," reprinted in Deutscher's *Heretics and Renegades* (London, 1955), pp. 46, 47. See above, p. 38.

If you want a picture of the future, imagine a boot stamping on a human face—forever.[3]

Power, in short, is sadism; and sadism is by itself sufficient to sustain the three elites of the world in their tireless activity.

It is hard not to feel that Orwell is placing too much strain on even the most dogged willingness to believe the worst about the future, or about tendencies in the present, or about the notorious features of the recent past, like Stalinism in the mid-thirties and Nazism in the early forties. The mind rebels: hatred must surely have clouded Orwell's understanding. There may be much in *1984* that is brilliant, inventive, close to reality or what is implicit in reality. But when it comes to disclosing the causes of evil behavior, is it not safe to say that Orwell is not to be trusted?

I think the answer must be yes—he is not to be trusted. Common sense must have its way, and common sense prevents acceptance of sadism as a constant and sufficient source of action on the part of millions of men, hour after hour, year after year. There is no historical experience that would bear Orwell out. The worst Nazi lived on something besides cruelty. In so far as one can deal with the question of political motivation in the abstract, one must conclude that the heart of *1984* is unsound. Winston himself cannot believe the explanation given to him by O'Brien; but the reader is supposed to see that it is the very liberalism he shares with Winston that blinds both to the truth. However, liberalism—that is, in the form of generosity in interpreting human behavior—is not needed to reject Orwell's characterization. The same hard-headed realism that leads one to expect the love of power to be operative in the world of politics, or indeed in all areas of human life from the most domestic to the most spiritual, must also keep one from picturing that love in too lurid a fashion. Furthermore, other things—other vices, at the least—drive political men to evil behavior. So has it been; so, one assumes, must it always be.

To say this is nevertheless not to hold Orwell's achievement cheap. Any political scientist must find *1984* a rich and greatly suggestive book. Nor is it to endorse the position taken by Anthony West; sly references to indefinite aberrations provide no help in looking at Orwell's writings, *1984* included. On the other hand, Deutscher does give a lead that is worth following: Orwell obviously wrote *1984* in a terrible conviction of defeat. We depart from Deutscher, however, when he charges Orwell with being a "simple-minded anarchist," a childish rationalist, a "quasi-mystical pessimist" for whom the Stalinist Great Purges proved too much to take, and who fell into "the abyss of despair" be-

[3] George Orwell, *Nineteen Eighty-four* (New York, 1949), p. 266.

cause of them. Orwell was not at all simple-minded, and the Stalinist Great Purges do not, by themselves, account for his anguish. The story of that anguish is more complicated. I should like to recount a bit of it here.

II

From his earliest political writings, like *The Road to Wigan Pier* (1937) and *Homage to Catalonia* (1938), Orwell is clear in his own mind as to the nature of his idealism. Nothing Orwell thereafter wrote indicated that this idealism had changed in the slightest way. Orwell died professing the only political faith he ever had, namely, faith in equalitarian and democratic socialism. The one thing that changed with time was the severity of his skepticism concerning the chances for realizing his kind of socialism. He was not at any time wholly free from skepticism; but in the last few years of his life that skepticism became deeper and deeper, and would seem finally to have extinguished hope altogether.

In a moving passage in *Homage to Catalonia*, a book written out of his experiences with the left-Anarchist forces during the Spanish Civil war, Orwell gave one of his best formulations of the socialist ideal. He is describing the "prevailing mental atmosphere" among the workers' militia in Aragon:

> Many of the normal motives of civilized life—snobbishness, money grub-bing, fear of the boss, etc.—had simply ceased to exist. The ordinary class-division of society had disappeared. . . . and no one owned anyone else as his master. . . . One had breathed the air of equality. . . . In that community where no one was on the make, where there was a shortage of everything but no privilege and no boot-licking, one got, perhaps, a crude forecast of what the opening stages of Socialism might be like.

Orwell distinguishes this socialism—authentic socialism, he called it —from the socialism of that "huge tribe of party-hacks and sleek little professors" who were busy proving that socialism meant nothing more than "a planned state-capitalism with the grab-motive left intact." [4] Orwell thus agrees with Malraux, who in his novel on the Spanish War, *Man's Hope*, has one character say that the opposite of humili-ation is fraternity: the substance of genuine radicalism is not only the elimination of poverty, but also of all the invisible barriers between men.[5] In any case, socialism is not in any important sense the quest for

[4] *Idem, Homage to Catalonia* (Boston, 1955), 104–5.
[5] André Malraux, *Man's Hope*, translated by S. Gilbert and A. Macdonald (New York, 1938), pp. 95, 207.

abundance and a life of self-indulgence, with all the state-control and planning that that would necessitate. Orwell was always more interested in abolishing extreme suffering than in imagining total felicity. In fact, Orwell thought that it was only after the abolition of extreme suffering that the "real problems of humanity"—the moral and spiritual ones—could fully disclose themselves.[6]

The enemies of this version of socialism were numerous, starting with the state socialists in England: *The Road to Wigan Pier* states Orwell's opposition to them at length and pungently. But there were other enemies, more dangerous and more hateful. There were the old-fashioned reactionaries: capital, the military, the church; there was the fascist movement culminating in Hitler, "the criminal lunatic," as Orwell called him in an essay on H. G. Wells written in 1941; there were the Bolsheviks who, in some ways better than the Fascists and Nazis, had nevertheless destroyed revolutionary idealism in the course of consolidating their power. There was, finally, the curse of ideology: the unreasoning attachment to the views of one's group, whatever the group, the blind loyalty to the group at the expense of the truth, at the expense of sanity itself. As Orwell puts it in his fine essay, "Notes on Nationalism" (1945): "the habit of identifying oneself with a single nation or other unit, placing it beyond good and evil and recognizing no other duty than that of advancing its interests." [7] It is in this latter essay, I think, that Orwell's hatred of the very essence of political involvement, of the very idea of organized solidarity in behalf of some worldly purpose, of the immersion of the self in something larger than the self, is most forcefully articulated, before the writing of *1984*. In sum, there was much to fill Orwell with disgust and anxiety in the late thirties and during the war. Indeed Orwell occasionally sounded beaten. In 1938, he wrote that "the one thing that never arrives is equality." [8] In his essay of 1941, "Wells, Hitler and the World State," Orwell said that H. G. Wells was too sane to understand the modern world, and that "a crude book like [London's] *The Iron Heel,* written nearly thirty years ago, is a truer prophecy of the future than either *Brave New World* or [Wells' own] *The Shape of Things to Come.*" [9] And in an essay published in 1943, called "Looking Back on the Spanish War," Orwell suggested that it was perhaps not childish or morbid to "terrify oneself with visions of a totalitarian future": fascism or "a

[6] George Orwell, "Looking Back on the Spanish War" (1943) in Orwell, *Collected Essays* (London, 1961), p. 206.

[7] *Idem*, "Notes on Nationalism," in *Collected Essays*, p. 265.

[8] Quoted in John Atkins, *George Orwell* (London, 1954), p. 13.

[9] Orwell, *Collected Essays*, p. 166.

combination of several Fascisms" could conceivably conquer the world.[10]

But for all the variety of terror and failure in the world of politics, Orwell did not give up. He retained a large degree of poise, even hopefulness in the period of 1936 to 1946. He continued to make distinctions between the different kinds of political evil: some were less terrible than other kinds; and, furthermore, some good things were within reach and should therefore be fought for. While the future could turn into an unrelieved nightmare, it need not. In a number of writings Orwell provided a corrective to his own despair and skepticism.

For example, he was ready as late as 1944 to claim that though "all revolutions are failures . . . they are not all the same failure." These words come from his quite acute essay on Arthur Koestler, in which Orwell tried to quarrel with Koestler's retreat from political life and with Koestler's oscillation between complete despondency about doing anything politically constructive in the present, on the one hand, and a desperate faith that sometime in the distant future the world will be Paradise because it would be intolerable to think otherwise, on the other. Orwell was interested in maintaining some middle ground, which consisted in valuing political activity without having any illusions concerning utopian success. What is more, he takes issue with Koestler's *The Gladiators* (1939), a novel dealing with Spartacus and the slave rebellion in Rome. Orwell seems unable to accept Koestler's view that when revolutions fail, the failure is to be attributed to the incompetence or petty selfishness of the masses. To the extent that *The Gladiators* is an attack on the ordinary lowly fellow (and I think Orwell exaggerates Koestler's tendencies in that direction), it is morally questionable and historically inaccurate. The struggle for power among the leaders, not the "hedonism" of the masses, wrecks revolution. Orwell says, "If Spartacus is the prototype of the modern revolutionary—and obviously he is intended as that—he should have gone astray because of the impossibility of combining power with righteousness." Orwell finds Koestler's *Darkness at Noon* (1941) to be a much sounder treatment of the perils of the revolutionary process. Orwell seems to endorse the principle that "revolution . . . is a corrupting process. . . . It is not merely that 'power corrupts': so also do the ways of attaining power." [11] Despite the force of that principle, however, Orwell does not come out and say that under no circumstances should

---

[10] *Ibid.*, p. 198. Toward the end of his long essay, "Inside the Whale" (1940), Orwell prophesies the death of liberal culture. "Almost certainly we are moving into an age of totalitarian dictatorships . . ." (*Collected Essays*, p. 157).

[11] *Idem*, "Arthur Koestler" in *Collected Essays*, pp. 225, 228, 232.

force be used to achieve social ends. Orwell's general critique of pacifism, which is carried on in several of his writings, seems to include a rejection of pacifism when it is used to undermine revolutionary exertion.

I would say that Orwell's fable, *Animal Farm* (1945), is his answer to Koestler's *The Gladiators* as much as it is a reworking of the themes of *Darkness at Noon*. From beginning to end, a love for the humble beasts informs the book; they work with incredible ardor, they hold on to a sense of dignity which taking part in the overthrow of the old order had first given them. They are, of course, victimized almost immediately after their initial success—victimized by their Pig leadership; and they are finally defeated: the revolutionary leadership turns into an oligarchy, the old oppression is conducted by new men, there has been little more than a circulation of elites. No doubt *Animal Farm* can be taken as a book preaching that "all revolutions are failures." The point is, nevertheless, that we must be clear as to what causes the failure; and we must acknowledge that on the way to failure a few excellent things can happen. That is, for a while, the masses may experience exhilaration and may attain to a fleeting self-respect founded on equality, though an equality of toil and scarcity. The residual feeling left by the book is not despair.

Another example of Orwell's composure at this time is his celebrated essay on Jonathan Swift, "Politics vs. Literature" (1946). The subject of this essay really is how an esthetic outlook on life can turn one sour and then reactionary. Orwell loved Swift, especially *Gulliver's Travels*, but, though loving him, took him for a great enemy of human progress. What Orwell wished to do in this essay, above all, was to champion the idea of social happiness against Swift's terrible *amertume*. We have already noticed that Orwell's idealism was not utopian: it held out no possibility that one day society could be perfect, that all the ills of man could be eradicated and that all the activities of men could be pleasurable. By "happiness" Orwell did not mean much more than the elimination of the worst sorts of avoidable suffering, the suffering brought about by want, class-feeling, and stultifying labor. Life could acquire *decency:* as Isaac Rosenfeld and others have said, that is probably the best word to describe Orwell's ideal.[12] And he found in Swift a venomous indictment of all mankind that would paralyze the effort to reconstruct society: how can you work to make men happy, or at least happier than they now are, unless you do not hate them? Orwell never said that the man of generous politics had to *love* humanity: that was for saints, that was perfectionism, and Orwell was, one could say, pro-

[12] Isaac Rosenfeld, "Reflections on Orwell," reprinted in Rosenfeld, *An Age of Enormity,* edited by T. Solotaroff (New York, 1962), pp. 246–57.

grammatically against perfection and sainthood.[13] But Swift's hatred
was corrosive; it had to be fought. Orwell did not scruple to psycholo-
gize at Swift's expense:

> The aim, as usual, is to humiliate Man by reminding him that he is weak
> and ridiculous, and above all that he stinks, and the ultimate motive,
> probably, is a kind of envy, the envy of the ghost for the living, of the
> man who knows he cannot be happy for the others who—so he fears—
> may be a little happier than himself. The political expression of such an
> outlook must be either reactionary or nihilistic, because the person who
> holds it will want to prevent society from developing in some direction
> in which his pessimism may be cheated.

Orwell thought the source of Swift's disgust was sexual impotence.
(How remarkably similar is Orwell's portrait of Swift to West's portrait
of Orwell.) The worst accusation that Orwell can make against Swift
is that his rendering of life on earth as hell is too partial: pessimism is
not adequate to all the facts. Orwell says: "Swift falsifies his picture
of the world by refusing to see anything in human life except dirt,
folly, and wickedness. . . . Human behavior, . . . especially in politics, is as he describes it, although it contains other more important
factors which he refuses to admit." [14] Those are the factors that make
for decency. They are precarious; their success is hardly assured; their
failure would certainly be assured if all good men thought—especially
if all good men felt—as Swift did.

The last example of Orwell's qualified optimism that I wish to refer
to is another essay, published in 1946, called "Second Thoughts on
James Burnham." This piece is important primarily because Orwell, in
the course of discussing two of Burnham's books—*The Managerial
Revolution* (1941) and *The Machiavellians* (1943)—attributes to Burnham a conception of politics which Orwell rejects, but which turns out
to be, in an intensified form, the intellectual basis of *1984*, published
three years later, in 1949.

Orwell finds that Burnham's theories are reducible to two propositions: (1) politics is essentially the same in all ages and (2) political
behavior is different from other kinds of behavior. Though Orwell's
handling of these propositions is not always clear, there is no doubt
that he finds them much too pessimistic and also lacking in historical
sense. He cannot accept the idea that love of power explains the fact
that human societies have been hierarchical down through the ages,

---

[13] See Orwell's "Reflections on Gandhi" and "Lear, Tolstoy and the Fool," both
reprinted in *The Orwell Reader* (New York, n.d.), pp. 328–35 and 300–315, respec-
tively.

[14] *Idem, Collected Essays*, pp. 394, 396–97.

with not only power, but also wealth and general well-being unequally distributed. Up to the present, scarcity would have dictated inequality, apart from the satisfaction inequality gives to men driven by the love of power. By making so much of the love of power as an ineradicable trait in human nature, Burnham forecloses the possibility of a genuine socialism. But, for Orwell, the great obstacle to socialism is not human nature as such; he seems to say that power-hunger is not a natural instinct like the desire for food, which "does not have to be explained." Orwell writes: "The question that [Burnham] ought to ask, and never does ask, is: why does the lust for naked power become a major human motive exactly *now*, when the dominion of man over man is ceasing to be necessary?" [15] He is prepared with the sketch of an answer: the "middling people"—the scientists, technicians, teachers, journalists, broadcasters, bureaucrats, professional politicians—want "a system which eliminates the upper class, keeps the working class in its place, and hands unlimited power to people very similar to themselves." These are the people, hungry for ever more power and prestige, who block the way to equalitarian socialism, who will try to prevent machine technology from making good its promise to rid the world of poverty and drudgery, and hence of the material preconditions of hierarchical rule. The implication is that though the love of power has always existed, it is only now that its consequences are of such magnitude. Furthermore, Orwell is certain that where love of power has dominated, as in the case of Nazi Germany and Bolshevik Russia, the political system is inherently unstable and doomed to extinction. If Orwell in 1940 and later could entertain the speculation that fascism might triumph on a worldwide scale, he is convinced, in 1946, that "slavery is no longer a stable basis for human society." The crimes of the Nazi leadership were also their follies; their suppression of freedom and decency had to lead to disaster, while "the Russian regime will either democratize itself, or it will perish."

Orwell is thus willing to believe that some men are in love with power; but he does not believe that they are now in control, or that the future could possibly be theirs. In contrast to Burnham, he refuses the temptation to generalize about political phenomena, and to generalize about them in a way most calculated to remove liberal and humane aspirations from the range of possibility forever. Orwell localizes his pessimism, as it were, even though he has often shown distaste for the behavior of political men. To be sure, the managerial stratum is troubling; but, says Orwell, "there is no strong reason for thinking

[15] *Ibid.*, p. 373. The relation between Orwell and Burnham is discussed in Michael Maddison, "*1984:* A Burnhamite Fantasy?" *Political Quarterly*, XXXII (1961), 71–79.

that [Burnham's theory of the managerial revolution] tells us anything about the future, except perhaps the immediate future." [16]

III

The question of questions, then, is, What happened to change Orwell's mind about Burnham's thesis? Why is it that writing in 1946, Orwell thought that the future would not be bad, as Burnham defined badness, but that in 1949, he could publish a novel in which the future is not only bad, but much worse than anything Burnham imagined. Burnham is content to explore considerations such as these: men of power look on policy as a means to get or hold power, rather than on power as a means to implement policy; men want power for psychological gratification rather than to promote substantive interests; the best metaphor for a political organization is a gang rather than an agency; and those in power look upon the governed as things to be used rather than as men to be served. Why is it that Orwell decided to enlarge on Burnham's thesis to the point of picturing the future as absolute evil? We have already noted that Orwell's health was poor; then, too, his wife died in 1945. Orwell was sick and gloomy; in 1947 he retired to a small farm on a distant, lonely island in the Hebrides, and cut himself off from society.[17] Personal facts obviously predisposed him toward looking at public facts with bitterness. But who can be satisfied with explaining *1984 simply* as the quite natural production of a distressed man? All that brilliance, all that ingenuity, all that power of rendering the intolerable must have come out of something political as well as something personal.

A clue to Orwell's thinking at what must be the time of brooding about, and preparing to write, *1984*—that is, the middle of 1947—is found in a short article he published in *Partisan Review* in 1947, called "Toward European Unity." In that piece Orwell lists three possibilities for the future: (1) a preventive war waged by the United States while it alone possessed atomic weapons; (2) the acquisition by the U.S.S.R. and other countries of atomic weapons, followed by atomic war, and the reduction of social life to a primitive level; and (3) a frozen *status quo,* brought about by the fear of using atomic weapons, in which the world will be divided into two or three super-states, each one of which will be a rigid hierarchical society "with a

---

[16] *Ibid.,* pp. 373–74. Also, see Orwell's essay, "Raffles and Miss Blandish" (1944), in *Collected Essays.* In this essay, Orwell raises the question of the relation between sadism, masochism, and power-worship (pp. 244–45).

[17] T. R. Fyvel, "George Orwell and Eric Blair," *Encounter,* XIII (1959), 60–65.

semidivine caste at the top and outright slavery at the bottom." [18]
Orwell thought that the third possibility was by far the worst, and the
one most likely. Only the spectacle of a democratic socialist society the
size of a united Western Europe could work to avoid the coming of the
totalitarian superstates. There were, however, titanic forces that would
oppose the creation of such a socialist society: the hostility of the Soviet
Union to a union of European nations not under its control and standing for values inimical to it; the hostility of the United States, as a capi-
talist country, to socialism; the remaining attachment to imperialism,
even on the part of the working classes; and the hostility of the Catholic Church, the inveterate foe of freedom of thought, human equality,
and the attempt to promote earthly happiness by social reform. The
future may turn out all right: things could change in Russia in a
liberal direction, America could go socialist when capitalism fails, as it
surely must; even in a world of superstates, the liberal tradition could
survive in the Anglo-American sector. It was hard to say; but "the
actual outlook, so far as I can calculate the probabilities, is very
dark. . . ." To these speculations, we must add that Orwell felt that
the Labor government had not taken any significant steps toward real
socialism; a few democratic reforms had been made, but they amounted
to very little. The English Left had missed the opportunity afforded,
first, by the war, and, second, by the accession of the Labor party to
power, to alter English life.

So that between the time of the essay on Burnham (1946) and of the
article just described (the middle of 1947), Orwell had abandoned the
view that the future was against the worldwide ascendancy of the
managerial stratum. Disappointment with the Attlee government had
combined with dismay at the beginnings of the cold war to weaken
Orwell's socialist expectations for the future nearly to the point of
extinction. That Orwell read the events of the postwar world with little
skill; that his understanding of American capitalism was minimal; that
his dislike of the American character prejudiced his predictions concerning the future—these things, I think, cannot be denied. The main
point is that with justice or not Orwell was sincerely persuaded, two
years after the end of the war, that though fascism had been defeated,

---

[18] George Orwell, "Toward European Unity," *Partisan Review,* XIV (1947), 347. It
should be noted that the superstates of 1984 come into being "after a decade of national wars, civil wars, revolutions and counterrevolutions in all parts of the
world . . ." (*Nineteen Eighty-four,* p. 206). Mention should also be made of the
similarity between the way in which the proles are treated in *1984* and the way in
which Hitler planned to treat the Slavs after Nazi victory. See Alan Bullock, *Hitler:
A Study in Tyranny* (rev. ed.; New York, 1964), pp. 693–703.

the potentiality for totalitarianism had not. America and Russia preserved that potentiality, and some decent alternative to both of them seemed implausible.

It must be said, however, that much as the Orwell of "Toward European Unity" differs from the Orwell of "Second Thoughts on James Burnham," one could not be prepared by "Toward European Unity" for *1984*. Orwell's novel goes beyond any pessimism contained in that short article, beyond any pessimism found elsewhere in Orwell's writings, and beyond—far beyond—the pessimism found in Burnham's writings, as well. The political situation accounts for much of the somber tone of "Toward European Unity," but it had not become so bad that *1984* can be seen as a reflection, though distorted, of it. On the other hand, all of Orwell's personal troubles taken together do not add up to *1984*; personal troubles never add up to a work of genius. What then is to be said about the genesis of this book? A possible answer is that Orwell consciously decided to become Jonathan Swift, only a Swift whose vision of horror would energize men rather than enervate them, a radical rather than a reactionary Swift.

IV

In his essay on Swift—to which we have already referred—Orwell concludes by explaining why he loved so deeply such a terribly reactionary writer. Orwell acknowledges that Swift was a thoroughgoing simplifier, a man who seized on one aspect of human life—its cruelty, dirt, and deformity—and wrote as if that aspect were the whole of life. Despite his one-sidedness, people respond to Swift; we all have moods which can be satisfied only by the most savage assaults on the life we live. Orwell says: "Swift did not possess ordinary wisdom, but he did possess a terrible intensity of vision, capable of picking out a single hidden truth and then magnifying it and distorting it." [19] The same description could be more or less made of Orwell's last book. (It would be a nice romanticism to believe that Orwell, a sick man, knew that *1984* would be his last book, and that he intended it as his testament.) We could say that Orwell deliberately sacrificed ordinary wisdom in order to achieve an intensity of vision. And he desired to achieve an intensity of vision, in order to rouse men to danger. What he did was to imagine a world in which everything he hated had coalesced and become omnipotent. The superstates of *1984* combine the overt features and implicit tendencies of Bolshevism, Capitalism, Imperialism, Nazism, and Roman Catholicism, plus a few resemblances to the an-

[19] Orwell, "Politics vs. Literature," p. 398.

cient slave societies, Platonic utopianism, and the dynastic politics of early modern Europe. Also included are references to the characteristics of all organizational life. Some features are copied fairly faithfully; some are exaggerated, or "magnified," to use Orwell's word about Swift. The system as a whole is endowed with a coherence that no system in the real world has ever had. Orwell asked himself the sociological question, What are the institutions required for a group of men in the modern world to wield absolute power? and the answer comes out in every detail, major and minor, of *1984*. In that respect, the book is a *tour de force,* one of the most successful acts of political imagination ever made. Reading it, one is thereafter made sensitive to any happening in the world that resembles, even slightly, something in *1984*; one is also equipped to examine dictatorships and oligarchies, past and present, with a heightened understanding. One's perception of even normal politics is altered. *1984* is a splendid work in defense of freedom and of equality. By predicting the future it may help to defeat its predictions; for that tactic to work, exaggeration is probably necessary. An image of pure evil must be presented, in order to sicken the decent man and make him more passionate in his attachment to the kinds of political good he still may be fortunate enough to enjoy.

The only question is whether the psychological foundations of *1984* detract from the book's hortatory value. We return to the motivation of the Inner Party: Can sadism sustain millions of men for a lifetime, generation after generation? When Burnham talked about the motivation of the managers, he did attribute to them a love of power; but that love is not made out to look like sadism: the love of control and initiative is not rendered as the love of inflicting pain. Besides, Burnham assumed that the managers want other satisfactions than those given by power. Orwell is, therefore, no student of Burnham, when he describes the mind of O'Brien. Granted that Orwell distorts for the sake of effect, is O'Brien's motivation, in fact, a distortion of some main characteristic of the political systems he hated? Studies in the psychology of despotic and totalitarian leadership are not far advanced, but there would seem to be little in them to match Orwell's analysis. The most stimulating works on this subject—Rauschning's *The Revolution of Nihilism,* Trevor-Roper's *The Last Days of Hitler,* Hannah Arendt's *The Origins of Totalitarianism* and *Eichmann in Jerusalem,* and Robert C. Tucker's essay on totalitarianism[20]—suggest that sadism

---

[20] Robert C. Tucker, "The Dictator and Totalitarianism," *World Politics,* XVII (1965), 555–83. It must be said that there are numerous and remarkable similarities between Orwell's book and Hannah Arendt's analysis in *The Origins of Totalitarianism* (New York, 1951). But there is one major difference. Miss Arendt says, "The aggressiveness of totalitarianism springs not from lust for power, and if it feverishly

is not by any means the sole ingredient, nor even a very important one. Fanaticism, adventurism, deep psychic impairment, cynicism, activism, nihilism, mindless loyalty—all these considerations figure; pure sadism, hardly at all. At the most elementary level, a distinction can be made between those who destroy in order to control, and those who control in order to destroy. If Orwell thought he was distorting rather than inventing, other writers would not back him up. Suppose, however, that it *is* invention, a departure on Orwell's part from recorded experience, in order to suggest the formation of a new kind of character, a kind that can emerge only when reality is prepared for it.[21] Orwell may be saying that there can be millions of O'Briens only when the material conditions needed for motivation like O'Brien's are on hand, when it is open to some men to control the behavior of other men absolutely. The opportunity will create the men—there is already enough evil in managers as we know them to assure us of that. Again, it is too much to ask us to believe that even in some future time, when conditions are yet more propitious for malevolence, a ruling class can live on hatred, can live without some other source of energy, some lie or self-deception, some trace of (perverted) humanity. Surely Orwell understood that. Furthermore, Orwell himself has not really answered the question he put to Burnham, the question he puts in Winston's mouth; he does not fully explain why men want power. All he does is to say that men want power in order to control men, and that control is best understood as the capacity to inflict pain, to make men suffer, and to change their behavior by means of suffering. He does not explain why some men want to make other men suffer. He does not even extend the line of inquiry suggested by, say, Harold Lasswell in *Power and Personality*. Lasswell writes, "Our key hypothesis about the power seeker is that he pursues power as a means of compensation against deprivation. *Power is expected to overcome low estimates of the self,* by changing either the traits of the self or the environment in which it functions." [22] Love of prestige draws men to power; concern for prestige profoundly influences the way men use power.

---

seeks to expand, it does so neither for expansion's sake nor for profit, but only for ideological reasons: to make the world consistent, to prove that its respective super-sense has been right" (p. 432).

[21] Irving Howe says, in his excellent essay, that "it is extremely important to note that the world of 1984 is *not* totalitarianism as we know it, but totalitarianism after its world triumph. Strictly speaking, the society of Oceania might be called post-totalitarian." "Orwell: History as Nightmare," in Howe, *Politics and the Novel* (New York, 1957), p. 250. See above, p. 53. See also Philip Rieff, "George Orwell and the Post-Liberal Imagination," *The Kenyon Review*, XVI (1954), 49–70.

[22] Harold Lasswell, *Power and Personality* (New York, 1962), p. 39.

The best Orwell can do is to suggest that wielding power as a member of a collectivity is a flight from the private, fragile, mortal self. In his essay of 1943, "Looking Back on the Spanish War," Orwell said that "the major problem of our time is the decay of the belief in personal immortality. . . ." And in "Notes on Nationalism," he said that, in his extended sense of the word, the worst traits of nationalism "have been made possible by the breakdown of patriotism and religious belief." [23] O'Brien develops this theme in the lessons he inflicts on his victim, Winston. O'Brien says,

> We are the priests of power. . . . God is power. . . . The first thing you must realize is that power is collective. The individual only has power in so far as he ceases to be an individual. You know the Party slogan: "Freedom is Slavery." Has it ever occurred to you that it is reversible? Slavery is freedom. Alone—free—the human being is always defeated. It must be so, because every human being is doomed to die, which is the greatest of all failures. But if he can make complete, utter submission, if he can escape from his identity, if he can merge himself in the Party so that he *is* the Party, then he is all-powerful and immortal.[24]

But with these words the most Orwell has done is to suggest some of the favorable psychological conditions for single-minded adherence to a cause or to an institution. There is, however, no easy leap from a wish to lose oneself and to forget that one must die, to total inhumanity. Orwell implies that there is. For that reason, his explanation is lamentably incomplete; it remain fatally implausible. Orwell has failed to account for political cruelty; he has failed to show that cruelty is the secret of power.

What then can one say? The truth of the matter may be only that Orwell thought that the imputation of sadism would be the best way to induce a fierce hatred on the part of the reader. Orwell's terrible vision of the coming power elite thus probably derives from an artistic and political calculation. That it is, in my opinion, a miscalculation should not diminish one's reverence for the book. Orwell had no hidden wound, as Anthony West would say; he had no simple mind, as Isaac Deutscher would say. His libertarian fervor carried him away; but that, for the most part, is to our unbelievable advantage.

[23] Orwell, *Collected Essays,* pp. 206, 286.
[24] Orwell, *Nineteen Eighty-Four,* p. 267.

Orwell and the Techniques
of Didactic Fantasy

by Alex Zwerdling

"A writer's political and religious beliefs are not excrescences
to be laughed away, but something that will leave their mark
even on the smallest detail of his work."

George Orwell, "W. B. Yeats"

An artist with a strong political commitment and a didactic bent is
often treated simply as a *thinker*. His ideas are analyzed and put in
order; his essays and letters are scrutinized for direct statements of
political belief; and his imaginative works are treated as though they
were a repository of useful quotations and had no individual integrity.
This may be a legitimate way to approach a politically conscious
writer who has no serious aesthetic commitment, but it is useless as a
way of understanding anything which can also be called a work of art.
In analyzing such works, the problem is to see exactly how (and how
successfully) the writer manages to negotiate between his didactic purpose and the aesthetic demands of his form. His political object may
originally have determined his choice of genre, but the genre—which
has a history and a logic of its own—will subsequently shape that object and perhaps even alter it beyond recognition.

The conflict between political and aesthetic pressures is one of the
constant elements of Orwell's career. It helps to explain, for example,
why he suddenly began to write in a different form in the nineteen-
forties. Before the Second World War he had specialized in the realistic
novel (*Burmese Days, Keep the Aspidistra Flying, A Clergyman's
Daughter, Coming Up for Air*) and the book-length documentary
(*Down and Out in Paris and London, The Road to Wigan Pier,
Homage to Catalonia*). During and after the War, he abandoned both

"Orwell and the Techniques of Didactic Fantasy," by Alex Zwerdling. © *1971 by
Alex Zwerdling. Printed here for the first time by permission of the author.*

these forms entirely and turned to the writing of fantasy—to *Animal Farm* and *Nineteen Eighty-Four*.[1] It is unusual for a writer to give up a literary method which he has mastered to adopt an entirely different mode. This significant turn in Orwell's career raises a number of questions which have not yet been answered: Why did he abandon realism and documentary? What attracted him about fantasy and how did he plan to use it as a vehicle for his political commitments? What are the inherent problems of writing didactic fantasy and how well did Orwell succeed in solving them?

In his attempt to make political writing into an art, Orwell had used the documentary and the realistic novel to expose the evils of his society, yet by the end of the thirties he had come to feel that neither form was doing its job. Both were fundamentally rational and depended on the writer's ability to observe and record the events and characters of the real world with accuracy. Possibly the appeal to reason failed to convey a sense of urgency; and perhaps the accuracy of external observation merely made readers treat such works as travel books, as topographical descriptions of an exotic landscape. In any case, it was clear that both had failed to make the audience care sufficiently about the abuses they exposed. As Orwell wrote shortly after the War, "This business of making people *conscious* of what is happening outside their own small circle is one of the major problems of our time, and a new literary technique will have to be evolved to meet it." [2]

The history of the nineteen-thirties and forties added to this sense of the bankruptcy of realism and documentary for the politically committed writer. Could totalitarianism, genocide, the resurgence of dictatorship and fanatic nationalism, the revival of torture and political imprisonment be explained adequately in documentary fashion? The world had become profoundly irrational since Orwell's young manhood, and he felt that its blatant insanity could only be understood by venturing beyond the boundaries of reason. In the essay "Wells, Hitler and the World State," he argues that the sensible humanitarian optimist can no longer grasp contemporary reality. Recent history had

---

[1] I use the general term "fantasy" to point to an important connection between *Animal Farm* and *Nineteen Eighty-Four*, despite the many differences between the two books. They are, of course, related to a variety of traditional literary forms: animal fable, allegory, utopia and anti-utopia, satire, and science fiction. The essential similarity among these various genres, and between Orwell's last two books, is that all permit the writer unusual imaginative freedom and make even his most extravagant inventions legitimate possibilities.

[2] George Orwell, "As I Please," *Collected Essays, Journalism and Letters,* ed. Sonia Orwell and Ian Angus (London, 1968) IV, 270. Hereafter, this edition will be referred to as *CEJL.*

been dominated by primitive passions which benevolent rationalists like Wells seemed incapable of understanding: "The energy that actually shapes the world springs from emotions—racial pride, leader-worship, religious belief, love of war—which liberal intellectuals mechanically write off as anachronisms, and which they have usually destroyed so completely in themselves as to have lost all power of action. . . . Wells is too sane to understand the modern world." [3]

Orwell hoped to find, in the fantastic works of the nineteen-forties, a literary vehicle which would expose readers directly to the irrational forces that seemed to control the world. Clearly, he needed a form which would give him great freedom to invent, one which would rely on the power of his imagination rather than the accuracy of his observation. He wanted a mode of expression which acted on some deeper and more primitive level of consciousness than realism or documentary had done. He must have made this decision with considerable misgiving, however. Fantasy is an unpredictable force and not at all easy to manipulate in order to express preconceived purposes. It can become really powerful only if the artist relaxes his absolute rational control and allows his imagination a certain freedom to wander. That such relaxation of purpose did not come easily to Orwell is suggested by the difference between his first attempt at fantasy and his second. *Animal Farm* and *Nineteen Eighty-Four* are very close to each other in subject matter, and both use fantasy elements, yet the earlier book is obviously much more rigidly and logically organized than the second. *Animal Farm* is about some of the irrational forces which dominate the modern world, but it is a very tightly controlled book.

Orwell was essentially moving toward an interest in and a need for myth, and this need was largely created by his awareness of recent history. The power of irrational forces was evident not only in the actions of nations but in most forms of political behavior, and Orwell concludes in one of his *Tribune* pieces that "the world is suffering from some kind of mental disease which must be diagnosed before it can be cured." [4] The most disturbing symptoms which had revealed themselves in the past decade were the worship of power and the extraordinary appeal of political myths. These two forces were in fact connected, for the myths were necessary to protect committed people from the knowledge that the universal hunger for power threatened every political system, no matter how idealistically conceived. The myths of the perfect society, of the inevitability of human improvement, and of the possibility of achieving genuine equality were all necessary to hide

[3] *CEJL* II, 141, 145.
[4] "As I Please," *CEJL* IV, 249.

the new *facts* of tyranny, the return to barbarism, and the rigidification of social privilege.

All these myths came together for Westerners in the myth of the Soviet Union—the ideal socialist commonwealth. The exposés of the late nineteen-thirties were largely forgotten during the War, when Russia became the ally of Britain and America. The doubts about Stalinist autocracy were conveniently buried, to be replaced once again by the romantic fiction of the worker's state. The size of the British Communist Party, for example, more than tripled during the war years.[5] Such signs disturbed Orwell profoundly, for they seemed to present a clear threat to democratic socialism. The exposure of Stalinist Russia in the essays and documentaries of the previous decade had obviously not worked if all they had taught could be so easily forgotten or ignored. Myth was more powerful than fact in most people's lives: the writer must start with this basic assumption. Orwell felt that the myth of a socialist Russia worked directly against the hopes of Western socialists like himself: "Nothing has contributed so much to the corruption of the original idea of Socialism as the belief that Russia is a Socialist country and that every act of its rulers must be excused, if not imitated," he wrote in a preface to *Animal Farm*. "And so for the past ten years I have been convinced that the destruction of the Soviet myth was essential if we wanted a revival of the Socialist movement." [6]

Fire can fight fire; counter-myths can defeat myths. Orwell set himself the task of exposing the illusion that the Soviet Union was an egalitarian society along with the widely accepted idea that state ownership guarantees the end of privilege. He knew that he would have to find a counter-myth which would take hold of the reader's mind by replacing its rival, and that to do this his tale would have to appeal to his audience's most basic feelings. The idealization of the Soviet Union as a utopian society grew out of people's need to believe their highest hopes could be fulfilled. Orwell's fables in *Animal Farm* and *Nineteen Eighty-Four* exploit an equally powerful emotion: the fear that one's worst nightmares might come true. To deal with such elemental subject matter, he had to resort to fantasy; realistic fiction was simply unequal to the task. Only an anti-utopia could displace a utopian vision; only the fear of hell was as powerful as the need for heaven.

If Orwell's fantasies are to work as cautionary tales, they must make such a deep impression that they continue to exist in the back of the mind ready to be recalled whenever something in the actual world threatens to make them come true. In *Nineteen Eighty-Four,* for in-

---

[5] Neal Wood, *Communism and British Intellectuals* (New York, 1959), p. 23.
[6] "Author's Preface to the Ukrainian Edition of *Animal Farm*," *CEJL* III, 405.

stance, Orwell has tried to make an audience with little direct experience of totalitarianism sensitive to how living in a society of constant surveillance and control might feel. Only in this way will such people be able to recognize and resist its first encroachments. That much of the vocabulary of the book has passed into common speech suggests he has been extraordinarily successful in achieving his goal. "Big Brother is watching you," for example, has become a familiar slogan used to identify any attempt by the state or other forms of authority to invade human privacy. This must have been exactly the response Orwell hoped for. He wanted his audience to remember *Nineteen Eighty-Four* not so much as a *book* (with plot, characters, and the rest of the machinery of fiction) but rather as a *Gestalt*, as a coherent world whose entire outline immediately comes to mind whenever one of its elements is discovered in the real world. For this reason the political system in *Nineteen Eighty-Four* "is endowed with a coherence that no system in the real world has ever had," as one critic has argued.[7] The paranoid intensity of Orwell's vision is a product of his feeling that the modern world can no longer be understood by the sane man of good will. Its excesses must be exaggerated and distorted in order to be grasped at all. Furthermore, the separate elements of the totalitarian state must be seen to fuse and form an intolerable design. Otherwise they may be dismissed as fortuitous, isolated, and insignificant symptoms.

Orwell was drawn to fantasy not only because of its appropriateness for presenting the madness of contemporary reality but because it seemed to make him the undisputed master over his own fictional world. Despite its dependence on the imagination, fantasy can be turned into an essentially idea-dominated form. The fabulist has much more complete control over the content of his work than the writer of realistic fiction or documentary. His freedom of choice is unlimited, while theirs is hemmed in by the demand for mimesis or for fact. In the fantastic fable Orwell had discovered the logical genre for someone drawn both to the implicit method of fiction and the explicit statement of the political essay. It was a form controlled by thematic urgency yet expressing itself in images, a form which directed the reader's attention to meaning rather than plot. The writer of didactic fantasy faces a serious problem, however. As the *Oxford English Dictionary* notes, the predominant sense of "fantasy" is "caprice, whim, fanciful invention." Such narratives often give us the feeling of mere ingenuity and contrivance, and the reader responds to them by admiring the author's cleverness but refusing to trust his vision. The feeling of the writer's

---

[7] George Kateb, "The Road to 1984," *Political Science Quarterly* 81 (1966), 577. [See this volume, pp. 73–87.]

absolute freedom easily leads to a sense of his fundamental irresponsibility and arbitrariness. This is a problem which any serious fantasy must overcome.

Orwell tried to overcome it by deliberately keeping his fantastic invention close to real events. The revolution in *Animal Farm* is of course carefully modelled on the Russian Revolution, and the methods of the police state in *Nineteen Eighty-Four* would have been familiar to an audience which had recently fought against Nazi Germany. He worked hard to make the literal level of his fables recognizable. *Nineteen Eighty-Four* takes place in London, for example, not in some new fantasy city of the future. Its buildings, neighborhoods, and way of life are clear references to the familiar present. Only the telescreens and posters of Big Brother differentiate Victory Mansions, where Winston Smith lives, from a decaying block of flats in the nineteen-forties. Orwell would never have been tempted to describe the world of 802,-701 A.D., as Wells had done in *The Time Machine*. His use of fantasy is deliberately rationed, and within the fantastic framework there is a good deal of realistic observation. *Animal Farm* could only have been written by someone who had observed life on a farm and how animals behave very closely. There are no unicorns in Orwell's bestiary; his imaginative excursions never left the familiar world far behind. As E. M. Forster said of *Nineteen Eighty-Four*, "There is not a monster in that hateful apocalypse which does not exist in embryo today." [8]

Orwell knew that if he wanted to avoid giving the sense of arbitrary invention, he would also have to give his fantasies a paradoxical emotional plausibility. We must be able to feel that the reactions of a Winston Smith, a Julia, an O'Brien are conceivable human responses *given the conditions in which they find themselves.* This would seem to be one of the laws of serious fantasy, that its imaginary world must nevertheless have the inner consistency of reality. The events, the agents, the settings of, say, Kafka's "Metamorphosis" or "The Ancient Mariner" can be absurd or impossible, but the emotions of the characters must strike us as plausible responses to their situations. This necessity explains, for example, some of the unexpected shifts of tone in *Animal Farm,* in which the flat characters suddenly turn round. When Boxer is taken off to his death, his friend Benjamin, who makes a specialty of ironic detachment, is suddenly but convincingly transformed into a violent and distracted creature: "It was the first time that they had ever seen Benjamin excited—indeed, it was the first time that anyone had ever seen him gallop." [9] And in the scene which parallels

[8] "George Orwell," *Two Cheers for Democracy* (London, 1951), p. 72.
[9] George Orwell, *Animal Farm* (New York, 1946), p. 101.

the Stalinist purge trials, the whole tone of Orwell's cool and witty narrative changes to match the events: "And so the tale of confessions and executions went on, until there was a pile of corpses lying before Napoleon's feet and the air was heavy with the smell of blood." [10]

Such internal plausibility is a form of realism, and its complexity is likely to come into conflict with the working out of the author's political purpose, which usually demands a more rigidly schematized fictional world. We can see this schematization in the last parts of *Nineteen Eighty-Four,* after the capture of Winston and Julia. There is a general sense of stridency and hysteria in this section, a feeling that a willed reality is replacing a plausible one. Orwell himself blamed his illness for these excesses, but the problem would have faced him in any case. As he wrote to Julian Symons in explanation of the "vulgarity" of the torture scenes, "I didn't know another way of getting somewhere near the effect I wanted." [11] Orwell's didactic intent here conflicts with his awareness of the subtleties of human behavior. The particular exaggerations (O'Brien's superhuman insight and naked commitment to power, Winston's continuous naiveté and final abject surrender) are there because the thesis of the book requires them. Winston must break down completely and be left utterly without dignity; otherwise the totalitarian system Orwell warns us of would not seem threatening enough. O'Brien must know all of Winston's thoughts and manifest an incomprehensible power-hunger; otherwise the prospect of such men in control would not be sufficiently frightening. Yet this sacrifice of complexity and emotional plausibility finally works against Orwell's purposes because it undercuts the reader's involvement and trust. "We hate poetry that has a palpable design upon us," as Keats said.

The danger of fantasy as a vehicle for a serious writer, as I have suggested, is that it will give us just such a sense of contrivance rather than of inevitability and truth. Yet if some parts of *Nineteen Eighty-Four* seem mechanical, the book as a whole often seems just the opposite—obsessive and unwilled. The tight control and parsimonious release of imaginative energy so evident in *Animal Farm* do not characterize the later work. Orwell has transformed the genre into a semi-confessional mode which expressed his own deepest conflicts and fears. To read his letters, essays and journals of the nineteen-forties is to become aware of how concerned he was with the issues raised in *Nineteen Eighty-Four;* but the parallels are not limited to ideas. He allowed himself to use even idiosyncratic personal fantasies in imagining

[10] Ibid., pp. 71–72.
[11] *CEJL* IV, 503.

the world of Oceania and the mind of Winston Smith. Orwell's lyrical feeling for the English countryside, his love of the naturalness of working-class life, and his nostalgia for the world of the recent past are all transferred to his fictional character. So are some of his fears. It is worth recalling, for instance, that Orwell could think of nothing more terrifying than "a rat running over me in the darkness," [12] as he confesses in *Homage to Catalonia*. This fear becomes the basis of the torture scene in *Nineteen Eighty-four*: Winston too feels that rats are "the worst thing in the world." [13] In *The Road to Wigan Pier*, Orwell records that he is haunted by the memory of "servants and coolies I had hit with my fist in moments of rage" in Burma.[14] Winston has similar sadistic fantasies: "Vivid, beautiful hallucinations flashed through his mind. He would flog her to death with a rubber truncheon." [15]

These extreme examples suggest that Orwell has unbound the fetters of fantasy and that the independent force of the imagination threatens to break away from all rational control. As one critic has said, *Nineteen Eighty-Four* is "a utopian 'De Profundis.' " [16] Its horror is not manufactured but experienced; its urgency and sense of personal witness are unmistakable. This has not always been treated as a virtue, however. In his study of utopian fantasy, Richard Gerber insists that the genre cannot sustain Orwell's passionate desperation: "A utopia cannot bear such tragedy. A utopian tragedy tends to be hysterical or sentimental. Being seriously crushed by a utopian hypothesis is the sign of a morbidly brooding mind." [17] And Anthony West has argued that Orwell unconsciously constructed the whole world of Oceania as an expression of his individual paranoia. Orwell's childhood sense of inferiority (described in the essay about his schooldays, "Such, Such Were the Joys") is projected onto society as a whole: *"Nineteen Eighty-Four* is not a rational attempt to imagine a probable future; it is an aggregate of 'all the things you've got at the back of your mind, the things you're terrified of'. Most of these, in *Nineteen Eighty-Four,* are of an infantile character, and they clearly derive from the experience described in *Such, Such Were the Joys.*" [18]

To deny a writer the power of his obsessions is to idealize the cool

[12] George Orwell, *Homage to Catalonia* (London, 1959), p. 87.
[13] George Orwell, *Nineteen Eighty-Four* (London, 1965), p. 290.
[14] George Orwell, *The Road to Wigan Pier* (London, 1965), p. 149.
[15] Orwell, *Nineteen Eighty-Four*, p. 19.
[16] Richard Gerber, *Utopian Fantasy: A Study of English Utopian Fiction since the End of the Nineteenth Century* (London, 1955), p. 129.
[17] Ibid.
[18] Anthony West, "George Orwell," *Principles and Persuasions* (London, 1958), p. 156.

and rational element in literature at the expense of some of the darker
forces which also go into its making. A distorted, "unreal" fictional
world can have extraordinary imaginative depth and compulsive
energy, as a Swift, a Kafka, or a Lawrence makes clear. Once released,
however, the obsessive fantasies of a writer can not so easily be controlled. Like the sorcerer's apprentice, they begin by doing the master's
bidding but often end by engulfing and dominating him completely.
Despite these dangers, Orwell's use of childhood fantasy remains
largely purposive in *Nineteen Eighty-Four*. He is writing, after all, for
an audience which has not experienced totalitarianism but *has* presumably experienced childhood terror. He is not engaged in "a rational attempt to imagine a probable future" but in trying to give his
readers an inkling of how it feels to live in a totalitarian state. His
point is that such regimes do not treat their citizens as adults but wish
to keep them in a state of childish dependence. All significant decisions
are made for them by "Big Brother"; all independent actions are
treated as threats to the authority of the state. Oceanic society is like
an enormous family with the dictatorial parents in complete control.
Orwell's plot records the unsuccessful rebellion of a prodigal son, a
"stubborn, self-willed exile from the loving breast." [19] Perhaps he re-
calls that Hitler attempted to impose the pattern of the family as a
single closed unit on a whole culture: "Ein Reich, ein Fuhrer, ein
Volk." The "infantile character" of Winston's fears is central to Orwell's conception of how totalitarianism works.

Not all of the compulsive material reinforces the original political
purpose of the book, however. It seems likely that Orwell did not
intend *Nineteen Eighty-Four* to be as remorselessly pessimistic as it
turned out to be. His important essay on James Burnham, for instance,
deals with the prediction that an invincible state like the one pictured
in the book will inevitably come into being. Orwell is at pains to deny
the validity of this vision of the future: "The huge, invincible, ever-
lasting slave empire of which Burnham appears to dream will not be
established, or, if established, will not endure, because slavery is no
longer a stable basis for human society." [20] Yet *Nineteen Eighty-Four*
permits no such easy optimism; its slave empire seems both established
and secure, and the hopes for its overthrow (Winston's rebellion, the
actions of the proles, or even Emmanuel Goldstein's revolution) are
treated either as failures or as " 'opeless fancies." If the purpose of
Orwell's book is to make people able to resist totalitarianism by exposing its nature and methods, the utter defeat of his hero in chal-
lenging authority is hardly apt to strengthen their resolve. It seems

[19] Orwell, *Nineteen Eighty-Four*, p. 304.
[20] "James Burnham and the Managerial Revolution," *CEJL* IV, 180.

likely that his attack on Burnham is an attempted exorcism, for the instinctive pessimism he argued against so vigorously had always lived in his own psyche. It is worth recalling that every novel Orwell wrote is essentially about a failed revolution—the unsuccessful attempt of a character to break out of the restricting way of life in which he finds himself and to alter his condition. Orwell's pessimism was a reflex imaginative act for him; by comparison, his optimism was only an idea.

The fantasy elements of *Nineteen Eighty-Four* thus reinforce only a part of Orwell's political purpose: that of exposing the audience to the nature of totalitarianism. The more hopeful side of his political faith, however, is left without imaginative support, and the book inexorably moves in a direction far from its original goal. This does not mean that the release of Orwell's imagination has destroyed his book, though it may have altered his preliminary intention beyond recognition. The expressive component of his fantasy world must be judged not by whether it serves his socialist commitment, nor by whether it violates the traditional assumptions of a genre, nor even by whether his obsessions are "morbid." Nor does the persuasiveness of such a work depend on how closely its vision corresponds to reality. The essential question is whether the writer's imagination expresses something absolutely idiosyncratic, or whether his extreme distortions are recognizable to many readers and in some sense acknowledged as their own. The extraordinary popularity of *Nineteen Eighty-Four*—the fact that almost every serious reader knows the book—offers indisputable testimony that Orwell's obsession is shared. His vision is selective and intense, but it is hardly unrecognizable.

That Orwell has created an imaginary world which gives coherent shape to a set of powerful human fears does not, however, necessarily mean he has solved the inherent problems of writing didactic fantasy. The greatest difficulty facing the writer of fable has always been to make both the literal and symbolic level—both the tale and the idea behind it—come alive without sacrificing one to the other. To treat the literal level as a mere distraction or a necessary evil may make the writer's purpose more apparent, but it also transforms his story into the fraudulent picture language which Coleridge contemptuously dismissed as allegory. Whatever label one chooses to apply to such works, it is clear that they do not work through the reader's imagination and intuitive understanding, that they are essays in thin fictional disguise. At the other extreme, the writer of fable can surrender himself so completely to his fantasy world that his didactic purpose is overwhelmed by ambiguous literal detail. His problem in writing didactic fantasy, in short, is to make his symbolic meaning clear without making it obtrusive.

A writer with a strong political commitment may be unwilling to trust the essential indirectness of fiction. The fear that the reader will not understand encourages him to incorporate miniature interpretive essays into his narrative. This tradition goes back to the Aesopian fable, which usually ends with an explicit moral lesson. La Fontaine, while acknowledging Aesop as his model, made his moral tags cryptic, witty and demanding in their own right. He occasionally dispenses with the moral altogether, "but only," as he says, "where I could not bring it in gracefully, and the reader could easily supply it." [21] Yet if the reader can "easily supply" the lesson, he probably does not need to be taught it. This suggests that the more implicit kind of fable is limited to reinforcing traditional wisdom and is not equipped to deal with unfamiliar ideas.

Yet Orwell's political truths were not those of the audience for which he wrote. He felt he had a new tale to tell, and this fact should make his uneasiness with indirect fable more comprehensible. Orwell was seriously worried about the reader's freedom to make of his story whatever he wished, and he was particularly disturbed with the way both his final books were misinterpreted. Although he did not want to comment on *Animal Farm* ("if it does not speak for itself, it is a failure"), he could not refrain from pointing out the error of one common misreading: "A number of readers may finish the book with the impression that it ends in the complete reconciliation of the pigs and the humans. That was not my intention; on the contrary I meant it to end on a loud note of discord." [22] Much more disturbing was the interpretation of *Nineteen Eighty-Four* as an attack on the Labour Party, or even on the ideals of socialism. Although Orwell realized that his last two books—intended as leftist internal criticism—were likely to be used by conservative and reactionary forces, he was unprepared for the confusion they aroused on his own side. In a public statement which was printed in *Life* and the *New York Times Book Review,* he spelled out his purposes: "My recent novel is NOT intended as an attack on Socialism or on the British Labour Party (of which I am a supporter) but as a show-up of the perversions to which a centralised economy is liable and which have already been partly realised in Communism and Fascism. I do not believe that the kind of society I describe necessarily *will* arrive, but I believe (allowing of course for the fact that the book is a satire) that something resembling it *could* arrive." [23]

Such explanatory statements, it must be remembered, are taken from prefaces and letters, not from the works themselves. This respect

[21] Jean de la Fontaine, *Fables,* trans. Edward Marsh (London, 1952), p. xiii.
[22] "Author's Preface to the Ukrainian Edition of *Animal Farm,*" *CEJL* III, 406.
[23] Letter to Francis A. Henson, 16 June 1949, *CEJL* IV, 502.

for the integrity of the fictional creation is much more severely strained in *Nineteen Eighty-Four* than in *Animal Farm,* however. In the later book, Orwell finds a way of incorporating the interpretive essay into the fantasy through the device of including passages from Emmanuel Goldstein's "The Theory and Practice of Oligarchical Collectivism," a work which analyzes the theoretical foundations of the state Orwell describes so graphically. The selections from this book appear in the story like so many lumps in the porridge, and though they are brilliantly written, they can hardly help distracting the reader's attention from the narrative and diluting its force. This is particularly apparent when the climactic and moving scene of Winston's conversion to love of Big Brother is followed by the appendix called "The Principles of Newspeak." Such essays are an attempt to solve one of the perennial problems of Orwell's fiction: his deliberate use of central characters whose awareness is more limited than his own. The disparity between the mind of the author and the consciousness of his major character is, in effect, distilled to form the essays. Orwell gives up the attempt to make emotional and intellectual sense simultaneously and relegates the two aspects of his book to separate sections. He was aware of the price of such a split yet could find no more satisfactory solution to this inherent problem of didactic fantasy.

Orwell's decision to provide such explicit interpretive help may have been based on the confusion created by *Animal Farm.* He must have felt that too many intelligent readers had failed to grasp his didactic purpose.[24] Despite the idiosyncratic interpretation of *Nineteen Eighty-Four* as an attack on the Labour Party, it created far less critical confusion than the earlier work. This was due not only to the incorporation of a reliable interpreter (Goldstein) into the book itself, but to the decision not to base the literal level of the story so exclusively on the factual details of a real state. The society of *Nineteen Eighty-Four* is more of an amalgam of different totalitarian and proto-totalitarian regimes. Its invention is, I think, a much more independent imaginative act than the working out of the story line of *Animal Farm.* The incidents of *Animal Farm* are largely selected from Soviet history and then translated into the terms of Orwell's story. Like a work of history, the book records a considerable period of time in strict chronological order. By comparison, the society of *Nineteen Eighty-Four* begins and ends as an accomplished fact, and its history is far from being the book's central concern. Furthermore, the relative freedom from precise historical parallels makes the later book less of a coterie work. Al-

---

[24] See, for example, Kingsley Martin, "Soviet Satire," *New Statesman and Nation,* 8 September 1945, p. 166; and Anthony Lewis, "T. S. Eliot and 'Animal Farm,'" *New York Times Book Review,* 26 January 1969, p. 16.

though it may not be necessary to know Soviet history to understand *Animal Farm,* one of the pleasures of reading it certainly lies in the prepared reader's recognition of Orwell's ingenious transformation of fact into fiction. It is more likely to appeal to a knowledgeable and sophisticated reader than to someone who is ignorant of the facts to which the book constantly refers. This is much less true of *Nineteen Eighty-Four* and helps to explain its wider audience and greater influence.

Animal Farm is short because it is essentially allusive. It depends on outside knowledge to give its fictive world resonance. In deciding not to rely on his audience's preparedness, Orwell was obliged to create a total world in *Nineteen Eighty-Four,* every detail of which he would have to illustrate. This is clearly a much more difficult imaginative undertaking and one which he accomplished with remarkable success. He made it an even harder one by refusing to rely on the exotic or bizarre. Many of his predecessors in the art of inventing future societies had concentrated on scientific advances. A major portion of Wells's *The Sleeper Awakes,* for example, is taken up with descriptions of the technology of the future. The reader who is not scientifically versed is obliged to take all this on faith and cannot connect it with elements of his own experience. By comparison, Orwell's descriptions of the future lay very little stress on technological changes, and his external world remains largely recognizable. What has been transformed is human behavior and institutions—a subject on which every man is an expert. His job is to convince the reader that the whole pattern of human life in his imagined world is simultaneously new and recognizable, and that it coheres.

He accomplishes this task by thrusting the reader into his world directly, without introduction. The fictive device of Wells's Time Traveller or Sleeper as well as all the other methods which utopia writers have used to bridge the gap between the present and the future —to ease the reader into the new society and give his temporary confusion a spokesman—are ruthlessly abandoned. The whole world of *Nineteen Eighty-Four* is simply treated as a given from the opening sentence of the book, and the unprepared reader is forced to make sense of it as he goes along. Much will at first seem incomprehensible to him. The society of the future is initially presented as an emotional reality in the consciousness of the book's major character, who is a citizen of that society. The train of thought we are asked to follow is small-scale and experiential rather than historical and theoretical. Both history and theory are there as well, but they come later in the reader's appropriation of the book.

It should be clear that this method is highly uncharacteristic of didactic writing, and that for all of Orwell's anxiety to control the interpretation of his work, he is ready enough to rely on the reader's blind response at crucial points in his narrative. He is willing to use a technique of literature which does *not* have a "palpable design upon us"—the slow unfolding of the author's purposes rather than their direct presentation. Orwell was in fact torn between these two literary methods, implicit and explicit, mysterious and schematic. Although he was drawn to propaganda, he knew that no propagandistic work was likely to last, no matter how powerfully it might affect its immediate audience. And he understood that to exert the kind of influence which interested him by this stage in his career he would have to work through the imagination and the emotions of his readers. To change their minds was an easier task than to shape their feelings, but the second was the more significant (and permanent) transformation. Despite all his doubts about the efficacy of fiction for political purposes, Orwell came to realize that he would have to trust its slow and unpredictable power. He did so to the limits of his ability, and he hoped that the dense literal reality which he had permitted himself to imagine in *Nineteen Eighty-Four* would sink into the consciousness of his readers whether they perfectly understood the book's theoretical implications or not.

It is tempting to see Orwell's achievement in writing didactic fantasy as the resolution of the life-long conflict between his political commitment and his artistic conscience. He says that *Animal Farm* was the first book in which he tried "to fuse political purpose and artistic purpose into one whole," [25] but the attempt to make a seamless garment of these two pieces of cloth certainly obsessed him at every stage of his career. It was responsible for all of Orwell's experiments in form, and the difficulty of the task he set himself helps to explain why so many of his works later struck him as failures. In nearly everything he wrote, we have the sense of a troubled consciousness attempting to find a vehicle of expression which would accommodate all of his complex needs as an artist, as a political thinker and as a human being. It is perhaps our sense of the ambitiousness and inherent difficulty of this attempt that makes us discount some of the obvious imperfections of Orwell's work and see the career itself as more successful and impressive than the individual works it produced.

[25] "Why I Write," *CEJL* I, 7.

PART THREE

View Points

Aldous Huxley: Letter to George Orwell

Dear Mr. Orwell,

It was very kind of you to tell your publishers to send me a copy of your book. It arrived as I was in the midst of a piece of work that required much reading and consulting of references; and since poor sight makes it necessary for me to ration my reading, I had to wait a long time before being able to embark on *Nineteen Eighty-Four.* Agreeing with all that the critics have written of it, I need not tell you, yet once more, how fine and how profoundly important the book is. May I speak instead of the thing with which the book deals—the ultimate revolution? The first hints of a philosophy of the ultimate revolution —the revolution which lies beyond politics and economics, and which aims at the total subversion of the individual's psychology and physiology—are to be found in the Marquis de Sade, who regarded himself as the continuator, the consummator, of Robespierre and Babeuf. The philosophy of the ruling minority in *Nineteen Eighty-Four* is a sadism which has been carried to its logical conclusion by going beyond sex and denying it. Whether in actual fact the policy of the boot-on-the-face can go on indefinitely seems doubtful. My own belief is that the ruling oligarchy will find less arduous and wasteful ways of governing and of satisfying its lust for power, and that these ways will resemble those which I described in *Brave New World.* I have had occasion recently to look into the history of animal magnetism and hypnotism, and have been greatly struck by the way in which, for a hundred and fifty years, the world has refused to take serious cognizance of the discoveries of Mesmer, Braid, Esdaile and the rest. Partly because of the prevailing materialism and partly because of prevailing respectability, nineteenth-century philosophers and men of science were not willing to investigate the odder facts of psychology. Consequently there was no pure science of psychology for practical men, such as politicians, soldiers and policemen, to apply in the field of government. Thanks to the voluntary ignorance of our fathers, the advent of the ultimate

From The Letters of Aldous Huxley, *edited by Grover Smith (New York: Harper & Row, Publishers, 1969), pp. 604–5. Copyright © 1969 by Laura Huxley. Reprinted by permission of Laura Huxley and the Library of University College, London.*

revolution was delayed for five or six generations. Another lucky accident was Freud's inability to hypnotize successfully and his consequent disparagement of hypnotism. This delayed the general application of hypnotism to psychiatry for at least forty years. But now psycho-analysis is being combined with hypnosis; and hypnosis has been made easy and indefinitely extensible through the use of barbiturates, which induce a hypnoid and suggestible state in even the most recalcitrant subjects. Within the next generation I believe that the world's rulers will discover that infant conditioning and narco-hypnosis are more efficient, as instruments of government, than clubs and prisons, and that the lust for power can be just as completely satisfied by suggesting people into loving their servitude as by flogging and kicking them into obedience. In other words, I feel that the nightmare of *Nineteen Eighty-Four* is destined to modulate into the nightmare of a world having more resemblance to that which I imagined in *Brave New World*. The change will be brought about as a result of a felt need for increased efficiency. Meanwhile, of course, there may be a large-scale biological and atomic war—in which case we shall have nightmares of other and scarcely imaginable kinds.

Thank you once again for the book.

> *Yours sincerely,*
> *Aldous Huxley*

Herbert Read: *1984*

Orwell's last work will undoubtedly rank as his greatest, though I suspect that *Animal Farm* will end by being the most popular, if only because it can be read as a fairy-tale by children. But *1984* has a far greater range of satirical force, and a grimness of power which could perhaps come only from the mind of a sick man. As literature, it has certain limitations. Satire, as Swift realised, becomes monotonous if carried too far in the same vein, and he therefore sent Gulliver to several different countries where human folly took on distinct guises. Though both writers have in common a savagery of indignation, the comparison of their work cannot be carried very far. Fundamental to Swift is a certain *disgust* of humanity and *despair* of life; fundamental to Orwell is a *love* of humanity and a passionate desire to live in freedom. There is a difference of style, too, for though both practised a

---

"1984" by Herbert Read. From World Review *16, n.s. (June, 1950), 58–59. Reprinted by permission of the publishers, Routledge & Kegan Paul.*

direct and unaffected narrative, Swift's is still playfully baroque—or, rather, baroquely playful. A more useful comparison is with Defoe— and this comparison holds good for the whole of Orwell's output. Defoe was the first writer to raise journalism to a literary art; Orwell perhaps the last. One could make direct comparisons between their writings if it would serve any purpose (between, say, *The Road to Wigan Pier* and the *Journal of the Plague Year*), but I prefer an indirect comparison between *1984* and *Robinson Crusoe.* The desert island is a long way from the totalitarian State; nevertheless, there is the same practicality in the construction of both books, and Winston Smith, "his chin nuzzled into his breast in an effort to escape the vile wind," slipping "quickly through the glass doors of Victory Mansions, though not quickly enough to prevent a swirl of gritty dust from entering along with him," is the same Little Man hero who, as Robinson Crusoe, being one day at Hull, "went on board a ship bound for London . . . without any consideration of circumstances or consequences, and in an ill hour, God knows." Strictly speaking, *Robinson Crusoe* is neither a satire nor an Utopia, whereas *1984* is an Utopia in reverse— not an *Erewhon,* which is an Utopia upside-down. *Erewhon* is still written after the ameliorative pattern of *Utopia* itself: you may, paradoxically, be punished for being ill, but the ideal is health. In *1984* the pattern is malevolent; everything is for the worst in the worst of all possible worlds. But the pattern begins in the present—in our existing totalitarian States.

On page *157* there is a significant sentence which might be taken as the motif of the book: *By lack of understanding they remained sane.* The crime of Winston Smith, the hero of *1984,* was the use of a critical intelligence, his Socratic inability to stop asking questions. That "ignorance is bliss" is no new discovery, but it has generally been assumed that understanding, which brings with it a sense of responsibility, an awareness of suffering and a tragic view of life, has compensations of a spiritual nature. It has been the object of modern tyrannies to deny man this sense of responsibility, and gradually to eliminate all feelings. The greatest enemies of the totalitarian State are not ideas (which can be dealt with dialectically) but aesthetic and erotic sensations. In the love of objective beauty, and in the love of an individual of the opposite sex, the most oppressed slave can escape to a free world. Religion is not so dangerous because it tends to be ideological and can be undermined by propaganda. But the sympathy of love, and the empathy of art—these feelings must be eradicated from the human breast if man's allegiance to Caesar (Big Brother) is to be complete. Orwell does not deal with the totalitarian hostility to art, but the dramatic quality which makes his satire so readable is due to his perception of the totalitarian hostility to love. " 'They can't get inside you,' she had said. But they could get inside you. 'What happens to you here is *for ever*,' O'Brien had said. That was a true word. There were things, your own acts, from which you could not recover. Something was killed in your breast: burnt out, cauterised out."

Orwell was a humanitarian—always moved by sympathy, by human love. The inconsistencies of his political opinions sprang from this fact. Consistently he would have been a pacifist, but he could not resist the Quixotic impulse to spring to arms in defence of the weak or oppressed. It would be difficult to say what positive political ideals were left this side of his overwhelming disillusion with Communism. In his last years he saw only the menace of the totalitarian State, and he knew he had only the force left to warn us. It is the most terrifying warning that a man has ever uttered, and its fascination derives from its veracity. Millions of people have read this book. Why? It has no charm; it makes no concession to sentiment. It is true that there are some traces of eroticism, but surely not enough to make the book, for those who seek that sort of thing, a worthwhile experience. An element of sado-masochism in the public may explain the strange success of this book. In the past the success of a book like Foxe's *Book of Martyrs* was not due to a disinterested love of the truth, or even to a hatred of Catholicism. Foxe himself was a tolerant man, but there is no evidence that his book produced a mood of tolerance in his millions of readers. I would like to think that the reading of *1984* had effectively turned the tide against the authoritarian State, but I see no evidence of it. Of Orwell's readers must it also be said: By lack of understanding they remain sane?

Wyndham Lewis: Climax and Change

At last, in 1945, Orwell's literary ambition was realized. He wrote a good book, *Animal Farm*.

As this is not literary criticism, I need not say very much as to the literary quality either of *Animal Farm* or *1984*. Treating of a society of animals, the theme brings to mind the classical masterpieces, which might, one would say, have inspired him to stylistic emulation. But this is not the case. The language is business-like and adequate but

"Climax and Change" by Wyndham Lewis. From The Writer and the Absolute *(London: Methuen & Co., Ltd., 1952), pp. 189–93. Reprinted by permission of Mrs. Wyndham Lewis.*

that is all. It is, however, a considerable feat of political lampooning. It is direct and dry, often witty. His "All animals are equal, but some are more equal than others" is a splendidly witty climax to the law-giving of the Pigs. And this little book, this sardonic parable, was a turning-point in the reaction. He showed the same courage in writing this as he had displayed as a "fighter for Freedom" in Spain (which subsequently he found was not Freedom after all, but slavery). With *Animal Farm* he led the wavering lefties out of the pink mists of Left Land into the clear daylight. Few, it is true, can or will follow him very far.

But *Animal Farm,* by reason of its success, made it respectable to think clearly or to write without humbug, if a young man was so dis-posed. It was in a sense an iron curtain that came down on the period of literary fellow-travelling, the work of an ex-fellow-traveller.

But for himself, as I have just stressed, he remained with one foot on *The Road to Wigan Pier*: the other foot in that region which had been finally opened to him by those foreigners of whom we have read his unqualified praise. To the Europeans of course must be added Burn-ham, and all the Trotskyite intelligentsia of the United States.

1984 is Wellsian in form, Wellsian in the style of its writing, Wellsian in the colourlessness and anonymity of the personae. I have discussed already, in passing, the reason for the insignificance of the humans who supply the drama in *1984*. There is, in fact, very little drama, in consequence of the extremely unelectrical quality of the human mate-rial. O'Brien, one of the two principal figures, is an uninteresting business man. If all the other humans in Orwell's novels had not been of so uniformly devitalized and colourless a type, one would have as-sumed that in *1984* the human element had been keyed down to show off the inhuman inquisitorial machinery to best advantage.

The manner in which Orwell has utilized the knowledge he acquired of the Communist attitude to objective truth is admirable. His hideous palaces of Truth and Love are first-rate political creations. His elabo-rate bureaucratic monstrosities will quite likely one day be historical facts: this is one of those rare books in which we may actually be look-ing at something existing in the future. Those parts of Goldstein's secret text which we are shown are well written, clear, and plausible. The interminable torturing, culminating on the page with "I Love Big Brother," is impressively chilly and logical. However, O'Brien and his victim are a comic pair sometimes: I think of the part where he bends over the truth-loving Winston and says "How many fingers have I got?", and when the foolish Winston still insists on counting in the way he was taught to do in the good old days of "two and two make four," the button is pressed and he receives a slightly more agonizing dose of torture than the last time. Here and elsewhere mirth is induced instead of terror, partly because an acute sense of the ridiculous is not Orwell's strong point, and then since the human beings involved are prefabricated and bloodless, we experience no sympathetic pang.

The book as a whole is a first-rate political document. There is only one thing I am obliged to point out. The old London lying all around this floodlit bureaucratic centre, this almost balletesque survival, full of the "Proles" which are Orwell's speciality, does not (perhaps oddly) make the scene more real. It is unlikely, in a régime such as Orwell describes, that the millions of ordinary people will be left unmolested, treated indeed as though they were not there. The appetite for power involves the maximum interference with other human beings.

But the hero's Orwellian enthusiasm for the "Proles" ("Proles" meaning "proletariat") imports a silliness into this book which is rather a pity. It is a silliness of the author of *The Road to Wigan Pier*; and that is not the author who was writing *1984*.

This natural life surrounding the artificial lunacy of the votaries of "Big Brother" is the real, unspoilt life of the people: that is the idea. It is the hero's belief that out of these vigorous, sane multitudes will come salvation. O'Brien, the powerful Commissar, is able to read Winston's thoughts. He says to him, "You believe, Winston, that the Proles will revolt and destroy us all. This is an illusion. There is not the slightest possibility of their doing anything of that kind," etc. etc. etc. etc. etc. Winston clings to Orwell's sentimental fancies. It is really Orwell who is on the rack. But he obstinately adheres to his love of the proletariat, whereas he should in fact be loving "Big Brother."

So that my meaning should not be mistaken, I consider a South-side publican, a garage hand, a docker, a city policeman, a window-cleaner, just as good as a Prime Minister, a Lord President of the Council, an Air Marshal, or a Captain of Industry. But I consider Orwell's romancing about the former group an insult to them, for he really thought that they were marked off in some mysterious way from the second group, which they are not. The whole of the *Wigan Pier* business was a very stupid affectation. I explained this at the time I was writing about the *Wigan Pier* book, but it is best perhaps to remind you of the nature of my criticism. One feels in the case of *1984* that it is as though a lot of William Morris bric-à-brac had got mixed up with the hysterical realities of the ghastly time we live in. The gutter-songs of the London children—"Oranges and lemons say the Bells of St. Clements; You owe me five farthings say the Bells of St. Martin's"—echo romantically through the book. But the London that existed when that song was written is no longer there—was no longer there in 1930. The bells of the various churches rang out clearly once, when London

was quite a small place, and everyone was familiar with their chimes.
But this song is an archaeological relic; and to use such a song to sym-
bolize the vast and roaring megalopolis of 1940 or '50 is absurd.

So we have the Old and the New contrasted. The Wellsian nightmare of a crazed totalitarianism stands for what socialism becomes
when interpreted as Stalin has done: the delightful, old-fashioned
London of the nineteen thirties, 'forties and 'fifties, with its hurdy-
gurdies, its "Oranges and Lemons," and anything else you can think of
to make it like the London of Charles Dickens,—that stands for the
socialism of Keir Hardie, or Lansbury, and of Orwell. For if, having
seen what "State" socialism is apt to turn into, we still remain Socialists, then this is no doubt the correct symbolical contrast.

No one any longer believes in the *simpliste* notion of workers
charged with an easily recognizable identity, causing them to be as
distinct as though all manual workers had black faces, and all who
were not manual workers white faces. No one believes in the myth any
longer of all these black-faced people rising in revolt, killing all the
white-faced people and there being henceforth a black-faced world. No
one believes this because they know that it is not an ultimate division,
working-class and nonworking-class; that there are deeper divisions
which ignore these very superficial ones. They know that proletarian
revolt must be engineered by members of the middle or upper class,
who do this out of ambition. They know that when a revolution is
over most of those who were manual workers before it are still manual
workers; and few, if any, of the new leaders belong to the class of
manual workers. The Orwell picture is of a long-out-dated socialism.
His two humanities contrasted in *1984*, of, on the one hand, a virgin
virile world of workers, bursting with potential leadership, on the
other, a ruling class on the Stalinist party-pattern, is really socialism in
one of its XIXth Century forms (probably medieval and guildish con-
fronting the stream-lined, ruthless, efficiency-socialism of today).

I for one would have considered *1984* a better book had the "Prole"
business been left out, and a more realistic treatment of the probable
condition of the mass of the population been employed.

So, finally, I do not regard Orwell as *un malin* like Sartre, but a
parallel with Sartre's case certainly exists. It seemed necessary to Orwell, in the interests of his reputation, not to withdraw from his con-
ventionally leftish position. How conscious he was in following this
line I do not know. But it is (and this is my argument) a false position,
as with Sartre; and so, too, numbers of other writers obliged to toe a
party-line of *some* sort.

In these politics-ridden times writers experience irresistible pressures, this way or that. Yet this pressure in a still free community can

be almost as destructive as the writing-to-order in Communist Russia. Every writer should keep himself free from party, clear of any group-pull: at least this is *my* view of truth. My truth is objective truth, in other words. In England the entire intellectual atmosphere is impregnated with liberalism, or rather what liberalism transforms itself into so as to become more-and-still-more liberal. With us the pressure to achieve conformity is very great. Whether in the matter of costume, or hair-cut, or intellectual fashion.

Orwell possessed a very vigorous mind, he went much farther on the road to an ultimate political realism than any of his companions or immediate English contemporaries. But you have seen him noting the great advantage the political writer of European origin has over the Englishman. Orwell, I feel, *did* almost wrench himself free. But the whole of his history is one of misdirected energy, and when, at the end, he transcended his earlier self, it was still to retain a bit of the old sentiment, to show his heart was still in the right place, in spite of the cruel and horrible things he had said about "The Great Russian Socialist Experiment."

A. L. Morton: From *The English Utopia*

It might be thought that this book[1] represented the lowest depths to which the new *genre* of anti-utopias could fall, but the publication a year later of *Nineteen Eighty-Four* robbed it of even that distinction. Here we are introduced to a world divided among three "communist" states which exist in a condition of permanent war, permanent scarcity, permanent purges and permanent slavery. The "hero" of the book is employed in the Ministry of Truth, whose task it is not only to deceive people about what is actually happening, but continually to recreate the past so that it is impossible to discover the truth about anything that has ever happened. For these purposes a new language "Double Talk" is being evolved, in which "Thought Crime," that is to say any idea not in line with the policy of the state at any given moment, will become impossible. This goal has not yet been reached, and the hero does fall into "Thought Crime" as well as into "Sex Crime," that is to say into love or a rather shoddy substitute for it. It is worth noting that in Orwell's world compulsory chastity plays the same role

From The English Utopia *by A. L. Morton (London: Lawrence & Wishart Ltd., 1952). Copyright © 1969 by A. L. Morton. Reprinted by permission of the publisher.*
[1] Morton has been discussing Aldous Huxley's *Ape and Essence.*

as compulsory promiscuity in *Brave New World*—the object in each case being to prevent normal sexual feeling, and so to degrade sex that it cannot afford any basis for individuality.

As a consequence of their crimes the hero and his mistress fall into the hands of the Ministry of Love, where he undergoes months of torture, lovingly described by Orwell in great detail, and is finally released an empty shell, completely broken and stripped of any trace of humanity. The whole account, like *Ape and Essence,* is tricked out with a pretence of philosophic discussion, but as an intellectual attack on Marxism it is beneath contempt. What Orwell does do with great skill is to play upon the lowest fears and prejudices engendered by bourgeois society in dissolution. His object is not to argue a case but to induce an irrational conviction in the minds of his readers that any attempt to realise socialism must lead to a world of corruption, torture and insecurity. To accomplish this no slander is too gross, no device too filthy: *Nineteen Eighty-Four* is, for this country at least, the last word to date in counter-revolutionary apologetics.

This would be a sordid ending to a splendid story if it were indeed the end. But of course it is not. The very degeneracy of such books as *Ape and Essence* and *Nineteen Eighty-Four* is in itself a symptom of the approach to a new stage. Such books are an acknowledgement by the defenders of bourgeois society that they have now nothing left to defend, of the inability of that society to provide any prospect of life for the people, let alone any hope of advance. In this sense they should be called anti-utopias rather than utopias, since the essence of the classical utopias of the past was a belief that by satire, by criticism or by holding up an example to be followed, they could help to change the world. In this they have had a positive part to play, they have stimulated thought, led men to criticise and fight against abuses, taught them that poverty and oppression were not a part of a natural order of things which must be endured.

Nor is this all. We can see today in the building of socialism a transformation of man and of nature on a scale never before attempted. The fantasies of Cokaygne, the projects of Bacon, the anticipations of Ernest Jones are in effect being translated into facts in the Stalin Plans which are now changing the face and the climate of the U.S.S.R. Writing of only one aspect of these plans, Professor Bernal said recently:

> This irrigation and afforestation is an over-all plan covering the whole of the dry areas of the Soviet Union, ranging from absolute desert to very dry sandy steppe, and steppe liable to drought. The total area involved is something like two million square miles, twice the size of Western Europe, or two-thirds the area of the United States. This whole area is being transformed by three simultaneous and complementary operations

—an afforestation scheme, a hydro-electric and navigation canal scheme and an irrigation and soil-conservation scheme. Though separately administered these form part of one coherent plan.

This realisation of Utopia through the power of the working class, which the Huxleys and Orwells find so terrifying, is the vindication of the belief that has lain at the roots of all the great utopian writings of the past, the belief in the capacity and the splendid future of mankind.

To-day the long and honoured stream of utopian writers has entered and made a noble contribution to the great river of the movement for socialism. Today millions are convinced that Utopia, not in the sense of a perfect and therefore unchanging society, but of a society alive and moving toward ever new victories, is to be had if men are ready to fight for it. Human knowledge, human activity, science in the service of the people not of the monopolists and war-makers, are leading to a world which, while it will not correspond to the desires of More, of Bacon, of Morris, or of the unknown poets who dreamed of the Land of Cokaygne, will have been enriched by all of them and by the many others who have made their contribution to that undefinable but ever living and growing reality which I have called the English Utopia.

Chronology of Important Dates

	Orwell	The Age
1903	George Orwell (Eric Arthur Blair) born June 25 at Motihari, Bengal.	
1917–21	At Eton.	World War I ends, Nov. 11, 1918.
1922	Joins Indian Imperial Police. Serves in Burma until August 1927.	
1928–29	In Paris, working as dishwasher; writing. Returns to England end of 1929.	Wall Street crash, October 1929. Beginning of Depression. One million two hundred thousand unemployed in Britain, 1929.
1931	In London, living with poor; hoppicking in Kent; tramping.	Two million seven hundred thousand unemployed in Britain.
1933	*Down and Out in Paris and London* published (January).	Hitler becomes Chancellor of Germany, Jan. 30. Reichstag fire Feb. 27; Hitler suspends civil liberties. Persecution of Jews begins.
1934	In London, working as bookseller's clerk; writing.	Stalin's purge of Russian Communist Party begins.
1935	*A Clergyman's Daughter* (March); *Burmese Days* (June, but written 1931–33).	Germany reoccupies Saar, repudiates Versailles Treaty. Italy invades Abyssinia.
1936	*Keep the Aspidistra Flying* (April). Leaves for Spain, Dec. 15; joins POUM December 30 in Barcelona.	Spanish Civil War begins, July 18.

1937	*The Road to Wigan Pier* (March). Orwell wounded in throat, May 20. Returns to England.	Bombing of Guernica, Apr. 27. POUM suppressed by Spanish Communists.
1938	*Homage to Catalonia* (April). Orwell ill with tuberculosis, goes to Morocco for winter.	Chamberlain, British Prime Minister, meets Hitler at Munich, gives him Czechoslovakia, Sept. 29.
1939	*Coming Up for Air* (June).	Barcelona falls, Jan. 26. Madrid surrenders to fascist troops March 28, ending Spanish Civil War. Britain and France declare war on Germany, Sept. 3.
1941	Goes to work for BBC as propagandist.	Battle of Britain, summer 1940–spring 1941. Germany invades Russia, June 22.
1943	Leaves BBC, begins *Animal Farm*.	Italy surrenders, Sept. 3.
1944	Completes *Animal Farm*.	Allied invasion of Europe at Normandy, June 6.
1945	*Animal Farm* published (August).	Germany surrenders, May 7. British elect Labour government, July 26. U.S. drops first atomic bomb at Hiroshima, Aug. 6. Japanese capitulate, Aug. 19.
1946	Takes house on Jura, in Hebrides.	First session of United Nations General Assembly, London, Jan. 10.
1947	Enters hospital with tuberculosis, December 20.	Economic crisis in Britain.
1948	Continues writing; returns to Jura in July. *1984* finished (November). Suffers relapse.	British pound devalued. Communist *coup d'état* in Czechoslovakia. Russians close off Berlin to Western powers.
1949	*1984* published (June). Orwell enters sanatorium Jan. 6.	Chinese Communists proclaim establishment of People's Republic of China, Oct. 1.
1950	Orwell dies in London, Jan. 21.	Korean war begins, June 25.

Notes on the Editor and Contributors

SAMUEL HYNES is professor of English and chairman of the department at Northwestern University. His books include *The Pattern of Hardy's Poetry* and *The Edwardian Turn of Mind*.

ISAAC DEUTSCHER, a Polish-born political writer and editor who lived in England, is best known for his three-volume biography of Trotsky (1954–63) and his life of Stalin (1949).

IRVING HOWE, writer on literature and politics, is professor of English at Hunter College. His critical essays are collected in *Politics and the Novel* (1957), *A World More Attractive* (1963), and *Decline of the New* (1970). He has also written studies of Sherwood Anderson, William Faulkner, and Thomas Hardy.

ALDOUS HUXLEY, the distinguished English novelist, was also a writer on philosophical and religious subjects. His own futuristic novels are *Brave New World* (1932) and *Ape and Essence* (1948). *Brave New World Revisited* (1958) is a commentary on modern social problems.

GEORGE KATEB teaches political science at Amherst College. He has written *Utopia and Its Enemies* (1963) and *Political Theory: Its Nature and Uses* (1968).

PERCY WYNDHAM LEWIS, English painter, novelist, and essayist, was a strong-minded, independent proponent of unpopular opinions from the years before the First World War until his death in 1957.

A. L. MORTON, an English Marxist writer on political subjects, has written *The English Utopia* (1952), *Socialism in Britain* (1963), *The Matter of Britain: Essays in a Living Culture* (1966), and *People's History of England* (1966).

V. S. PRITCHETT, the English novelist and short-story writer, has also written several books of critical essays, including *In My Good Books* (1942), *Books in General* (1953), *The Living Novel* (1947), and *The Working Novelist* (1965).

HERBERT READ was a poet, novelist, and publisher who wrote widely on art and literature and was considered among the most important of modern English art critics.

STEPHEN SPENDER, English poet and critic, is currently professor of English at University College, London.

JOHN STRACHEY, politician and political writer, was the most articulate of British Marxists during the 1930s. His books, including *The Coming Struggle for Power* (1932) and *The Menace of Fascism* (1933) helped to alert the British people to the political issues of the time. Strachey was a Member of Parliament in the early 30s and from 1945 until his death in 1961. From 1946 to 1951 he was a Cabinet Member in the Labour government.

LIONEL TRILLING is University Professor at Columbia University. His critical writings include *Matthew Arnold* (1939), *E. M. Forster* (1943), *The Liberal Imagination* (1950), *The Opposing Self* (1955), *Beyond Culture* (1965), and *The Experience of Literature* (1967).

ALEX ZWERDLING, associate professor of English at the University of California, Berkeley, is the author of *Yeats and the Heroic Ideal* (1965). He is presently working on a study of Orwell, which includes the essay written here.

Selected Bibliography

George Orwell's occasional writings have been gathered together in the four-volume *Collected Essays, Journalism & Letters* (New York: Harcourt Brace Jovanovich, Inc., 1968). Many of the essays included there express Orwell's ideas about politics, writing, and the modern world and are therefore relevant to a study of *1984*. I particularly recommend the following:

in volume I: "Why I Write," "Charles Dickens," "Inside the Whale," and "My Country Right or Left";
in volume II: "The Lion and the Unicorn";
in volume IV: Orwell's review of *We,* by E. I. Zamyatin, "Politics and the English Language," and "Writers and Leviathan."

Orwell's pamphlet, *The English People* (Glasgow: William Collins & Co. Ltd., 1947) is also of special interest.

Critical Books

Atkins, John, *George Orwell.* New York: Frederick Ungar Publishing Co., Inc., 1965. A literary and biographical study by an English critic who knew and admired Orwell.

Hopkinson, Tom, *George Orwell.* London: Longmans, Green & Co., Ltd., 1955. A pamphlet in the British Council series; brief, but perceptive. Bibliography.

Lee, Robert A., *Orwell's Fiction.* Notre Dame, Indiana: University of Notre Dame Press, 1969. A defense of Orwell as a novelist against the common opinion that he is interesting primarily for his ideas. Bibliography.

Oxley, B. T., *George Orwell.* London: Evans Brothers Limited, 1967. A useful short introduction to Orwell, especially good on the historical context. Bibliography.

Rees, Richard, *George Orwell Fugitive from the Camp of Victory.* London: Martin Secker & Warburg Ltd., 1961. A book about Orwell's books. Rees was Orwell's friend for twenty years, and he writes with warm personal insight.

Thomas, Edward M., *Orwell*. Edinburgh: Oliver and Boyd Limited, 1965. Another short introduction (from the "Writers and Critics Series") emphasizing the importance of the essays and nonfictional writings. Bibliography.

Woodcock, George, *The Crystal Spirit*. Boston: Little, Brown and Company, 1966. The best biographical book on Orwell, by a friend who was also a political associate.

Critical Essays

Mander, John, "Orwell in the Sixties," in *The Writer and Commitment*. London: Martin Secker & Warburg Ltd., 1961. A thoughtful evaluation of Orwell's political thinking and the contradictions in it.

Trilling, Lionel, "George Orwell and the Politics of Truth," in *The Opposing Self*. New York: The Viking Press, Inc., 1955. An Introduction to *Homage to Catalonia*, which is also a tribute to Orwell's political virtues.

Wain, John, "George Orwell (I) and (II)," in *Essays on Literature and Ideas*. London: Macmillan & Co. Ltd., 1964. Essays on Orwell's social writings and his relation to the past by a gifted novelist who has some affinities with Orwell as a writer.

Williams, Raymond, "George Orwell," in *Culture and Society 1780–1950*. London: Chatto & Windus Ltd., 1960. A severe but just criticism of the paradoxes in Orwell's thought, and some suggested explanations.

World Review 16, n.s. (June, 1950). Essays and memoirs of Orwell by various writers, including Bertrand Russell, Malcolm Muggeridge, Aldous Huxley, and Stephen Spender. Also includes passages from Orwell's notebooks for 1940–41.

TWENTIETH CENTURY
INTERPRETATIONS

MAYNARD MACK, *Series Editor*
Yale University

NOW AVAILABLE
Collections of Critical Essays
ON

ADVENTURES OF HUCKLEBERRY FINN
ALL FOR LOVE
THE AMBASSADORS
ARROWSMITH
AS YOU LIKE IT
BILLY BUDD
BLEAK HOUSE
THE BOOK OF JOB
BOSWELL'S LIFE OF JOHNSON
THE CASTLE
CORIOLANUS
DOCTOR FAUSTUS
DON JUAN
DUBLINERS
THE DUCHESS OF MALFI
ENDGAME
EURIPIDES' ALCESTIS
THE EVE OF ST. AGNES
THE FALL OF THE HOUSE OF USHER
A FAREWELL TO ARMS
THE FROGS
GRAY'S ELEGY
THE GREAT GATSBY
GULLIVER'S TRAVELS
HAMLET
HARD TIMES
HENRY IV, PART ONE
HENRY IV, PART TWO
HENRY V
THE ICEMAN COMETH
INVISIBLE MAN
JULIUS CAESAR
KEATS'S ODES
LIGHT IN AUGUST
LORD JIM
MAJOR BARBARA

(continued on next page)

(*continued from previous page*)